The Ultimate Guide to Trading ETFs

How to Profit from the Hottest Sectors in the Hottest Markets All the Time

Don Dion
Carolyn Dion

WILEY

John Wiley & Sons, Inc.

Published by John Wiley & Sons, Inc., Hoboken, New Jersey.
Published simultaneously in Canada.

For general information on our other products and services or for technical support, please contact our Customer Care Department within the United States at (800) 762-2974, outside the United States at (317) 572-3993 or fax (317) 572-4002.

Wiley also publishes its books in a variety of electronic formats. Some content that appears in print may not be available in electronic books. For more information about Wiley products, visit our web site at www.wiley.com.

Library of Congress Cataloging-in-Publication Data:

Dion, Don, 1954-
   The ultimate guide to trading ETFs : how to profit from the hottest sectors in the hottest markets all the time / Don Dion, Carolyn Dion.
       p. cm.
   Includes index.
       ISBN 978-0-470-60437-3 (cloth); ISBN 978-0-470-91519-6 (ebk);
ISBN 978-0-470-9152-0 (ebk); ISBN 978-0-470-91521-9 (ebk)
   1. Exchange traded funds.   2. Stock funds.   I. Dion, Carolyn, 1983-   II. Title.
   HG6043.D56 2010
   332.63'27–dc22
                                                                        2010039911

Printed in the United States of America

10 9 8 7 6 5 4 3 2 1

To my parents, Donald R. Dion Sr. and Hilda Dion
—D.D.
To Pauline T. Dion and Tamara P. Carl
—C.D.

Contents

Preface

S ince their beginning, exchange-traded funds (ETFs) have been nothing less than revolutionary. Transparent, liquid, and low-cost, these instruments allow investors to take positions in underlying indexes as easily as buying shares in a favorite stock. No wonder their popularity spread among institutions and, increasingly, retail investors.

What no one could have foreseen in the early days, perhaps, is the magnitude of the impact ETFs would have on the investment industry. In addition to products that track the major indexes such as the S&P 500, NASDAQ, and Russell 2000, there are myriad choices across sectors and strategies, from the straightforward to the complex.

As of this writing, as recovery continues from the financial crisis that pummeled the stock market and bruised Wall Street as well, ETFs appear to be the right product at the right time. For investors who want to call their own shots, ETFs are a near-perfect solution. One major caveat, however, is that ETFs have become so popular, the playing field is crowded with potential candidates. Look-alikes and sound-alikes may potentially confuse investors who do not take the time to educate themselves.

In *The Ultimate Guide to Trading ETFs*, our goal is to demystify the process of choosing ETFs. Whether an investor is looking at the plain vanilla of an S&P fund or a more exotic offering in an emerging market, or to gain access to a commodity such as platinum or palladium, there are criteria to keep in mind: among them, liquidity, transparency, and cost. The number one factor with any ETF, as readers will learn, is that it must do what it says it will do—namely, track its underlying portfolio. Sounds simple, but not so easy to execute, as we have seen with a number of ETFs that suddenly develop steep premiums or deep discounts to their net asset values (NAVs). In order to avoid funds that are thinly traded, inefficiently priced, or fail to live up to their objectives, investors must empower themselves with the information they need to make smart choices. Our hope is that this book will provide that education.

Both of us have made ETFs a centerpiece of our professional lives. Don Dion is the publisher of *ETF Action*, and the president and founder of Dion Money Management. Working with clients in 49 states and 11 countries, Don has more than 25 years of experience in the financial markets, and is regarded as an expert in ETFs and mutual funds. He is also the publisher of the Fidelity Independent Adviser family of newsletters, which provide broad market commentary. For him, the combination of market knowledge, investor support, and education has been a longtime passion.

Carolyn Dion is an analyst and associate editor for the Fidelity Independent Adviser newsletters, and a vice president of Dion Money Management. Before joining the firm, she was an ETF market maker for Kellogg Specialist Group on the New York Stock Exchange and the American Stock Exchange. Her experience put her literally on the frontlines of ETF launches and trading, giving her a bird's-eye view of what distinguishes between a successful fund and one that fails to meet its objectives.

We bring together the best of our worlds in a book meant to enlighten and empower. Investors can make good decisions for themselves. It takes diligence and dedication, and it can be done. In the pages of this book, we hope you find your questions answered and your curiosity piqued.

Acknowledgments

We wish to express our gratitude to those who helped make this book a reality, especially:

At Dion Money Management: Matthew Cowie, Nicholas Botto, Jonathan Buoni, Matthew Sauer, and Dave Bogonovitch for their help and guidance.

At TheStreet.com: Glenn Hall, William Hennelly, Poilin Breathnach, Eric Harding, and David Tong.

At our publisher, John Wiley & Sons: Kevin Commins, Executive Editor, who encouraged us to take on this project; Meg Freeborn, Development Editor, for her assistance; and Tricia Crisafulli for editorial assistance to help make this book possible.

For Don, I would like to thank my partners at both Dion Money Management and Focus Financial Partners. Special thanks also to my friends and family.

For Carolyn, I would first like to thank Kirk Kellogg, Stephen O'Grady, and my former colleagues at Kellogg Specialist Group. Special thanks to Richard Farrell, Michael Feehan, Josh Rosen, Howard Shallcross, Daniel Madden, and Paul Shust.

This book would not have been possible without the support of my family and friends. Special thanks to Colin O'Connor, Theresa

Patry, Donald R. Dion Sr., Hilda Dion, Liora Hickman, Kathryn Swiatek, Jason Scherman, and Noah Kyman.

We would also like to acknowledge with gratitude the clients at Dion Money Management and our loyal readers at TheStreet.com. Your interaction with us every day reminds us why we are in this business.

Part I

ETFS: A NEW WAY TO INVEST AND TRADE

Chapter 1

Taking an Active Approach with ETFs

In the last decade, exchange-traded funds (ETFs) have experienced strong growth, offering increased access to the market through a host of new products. With advantages such as transparency, liquidity, tax efficiency, and lower costs compared to other instruments, ETFs have become highly appealing to independent-minded investors. Whether you are a sophisticated investor who is well versed in ETFs or you are a novice who is just becoming familiar with these funds, there is a wider range of choices today to help you put your investment ideas to work for the short or long term without relying on a fund manager as an intermediary.

Although growth in the industry is positive, it's important for you to understand that not every new offering is appropriate for you to consider. The surge in ETFs has brought a number of new funds and issuers into the mix, hoping to catch the wave of investor demand. Not all the products that venture out, however, will make it. Some will founder without sufficient investor interest to remain afloat. To keep your portfolios from being dragged under by poorly performing

ETFs, you need to be particularly discerning as you pick the exposure you want and when you want it; whether to a broad-based index such as the S&P 500, an industry sector such as biotech or retail, or a particular country or geographic region such as emerging markets.

Given the ravages of the 2007–2008 bear market on 401(k) plans and other retirement accounts, the attributes of ETFs are more important than ever. Having suffered through the market downturn, you may be among the investors who are reluctant to hand over complete responsibility for their financial well-being. Tired of being told that investing is the realm of professionals and beyond the capacity of the average individual, you want the process to be demystified. The good news is, with ETFs you have greater ability to accomplish on your own what you may have once thought was impossible without the assistance of a broker and an incredible amount of financial knowledge.

The increased popularity of ETFs is evidenced by the numbers. According to the Financial Research Corporation, ETFs have grown at a rate of 35 percent compounded annually since 1999.[1] Barclays Global Investors, founder of the popular iShares funds, reported that total global ETF assets swelled to an all-time high of $857.5 billion at the end of the second quarter of 2009. The previous record of $796.7 billion was set in 2007. Asset growth increased by 34 percent in Europe, 35 percent in Latin America, and 39 percent in Asia (excluding Japan where ETF assets declined 7 percent), while the United States saw growth of 17 percent. Although the rate of increase in Europe, Asia, and Latin America outpaced that of the United States, it is likely that as international markets mature, they, too, will see their asset growth slow. The United States, with ETF assets of $582 billion in mid-2009, the highest level since December 2007, remains a stronghold of ETF investing.[2] What these numbers mean to you is that, as

[1]FRCNet.com, "Marketplace Underestimates the Threat Posed by Actively Managed ETFs, According to Latest Financial Research Corporation Study," Financial Research Corporation Press Release, April 13, 2009, http://www.frcnet.com/Press_Releases_07/Marketplace-Underestimates-the-Threat-Posed-by-Actively-Managed-ETFs.pdf.
[2]Cinthia Murphy, "U.S. ETF Growth Lags; Fund Costs Are a Bit Better," SeekingAlpha.com, September 21, 2009, http://seekingalpha.com/article/162606-u-s-etf-growth-lags-fund-costs-are-a-bit-better.

an ETF investor, you are in good company among growing ranks of retail and institutional participants, which will help ensure a healthy investment sector overall for the foreseeable future.

Understanding ETFs

Even if you are aware of ETFs, you may not understand how they are structured. Essentially, an ETF is an investment product that allows investors to buy and sell shares of a single security that represents a stake or part ownership in a portfolio of securities, such as an index. The defining features of ETFs are that they closely track an underlying index or portfolio and that trade throughout the day at market-determined prices. These attributes contrast distinctly with mutual funds, which are bought and sold only at the market close, and with closed-end funds that may trade at a premium or discount to the value of their underlying portfolios.

Not all ETFs are the same, however, and some do a better job than others of delivering on their investment promise. Too often investors do not get what they bargained for when it comes to their ETF choices. Therefore, you need to know how to identify ETFs that really do work, meaning there is a close relationship between the fund's price and its underlying portfolio, as reflected in its net asset value (NAV). The NAV is calculated based on the total assets of the fund, subtracting expenses and dividing by the number of shares outstanding. The price of most large, liquid funds does not deviate much from their NAV, although supply and demand can create some fluctuations during the trading day. With a thinly traded, specialized fund, the price can be a significant premium or discount to the NAV.

ETF issuers charge a management fee, which is deducted directly from the assets of the fund. Therefore, the investment return of the ETF could be lower than the underlying index. Investors also pay commissions and/or transaction costs to a brokerage firm when buying and selling ETFs, just as they would with a stock transaction. Because ETFs trade throughout the day, real-time prices for these instruments are available during trading hours, similar to any stock quote. Originally, ETFs were marketed mostly to institutional investors who used them to execute specific strategies, including hedging. Today, as retail activity has risen sharply, it is estimated that institutional players account for only about half the assets held in ETFs.

For discussion purposes, most people put the launch date for ETFs at 1993, the year that the SPDR S&P 500 (SPY), or "spider" as it is nicknamed, was launched by State Street Global Advisors. Although similar products existed in the United States and Canada prior to that date, the SPDR is considered to be the granddaddy of all ETFs; today it accounts for more than $69 billion in assets and remains the most liquid ETF in the world. The launch of the SPDR, which tracks the S&P 500, on the American Stock Exchange boosted the prominence of that exchange and gave it room to flourish. Since then, the Amex has merged with the New York Stock Exchange, and ETFs now trade on a sophisticated electronic platform, the NYSE Arca electronic exchange. Arguably, these two developments have improved the efficiency of ETFs, further helping them to achieve their number one objective: trading at or near their NAV.

This is an important concept for you to grasp as an investor. The determining factor of what makes an ETF successful is that it tracks its underlying portfolio—not whether the price of the fund goes up or down. Don't fall into the trap of buying an ETF simply because the price is rising. That fund may not be the best investment choice for you because it is illiquid and tends to trade at measurable premium or discount to its NAV.

Since the beginning, more than 700 ETFs have been introduced, providing exposure to a wide range of investment choices including broad stock indexes, industry sectors, fixed income, international, and global. In addition to funds that trade in the United States, ETFs have also been created to trade in international markets. Among the most popular ETFs are those that provide exposure to broad market indexes, such as the PowerShares QQQ Trust (QQQQ), which holds the component securities of the NASDAQ 100. In addition, there are sector funds that are very large in terms of assets such as the SPDR Gold Trust (GLD), which gives investors exposure to gold bullion. Several emerging market funds, such as iShares MSCI Emerging Markets (EEM), are also among the top 10 ETFs in terms of asset size. While broad indexes are still among the largest, increasing usage of funds such as GLD and EEM prove that investors are using ETFs to slice up and gain access to smaller parts of the market.

One of the fastest growing areas of the ETF industry is fixed income. This may reflect the needs of baby boomer investors who are seeking an income stream as they approach or enter retirement years. Increasingly, older baby boomers are forming a larger demographic of ETF investors.

There are also variations in how ETFs are constructed. The original ETFs that track familiar indexes such as the Dow Jones Industrial Average, S&P 500, and the Russell 2000 are weighted by capitalization. New ETFs have been launched that track indexes that are weighted differently, such as on the basis of revenue or dividends. Recent developments in weighting illustrate the fact that, whatever investment objective you are pursuing, there most likely is an ETF to match.

In short, ETFs are nothing short of revolutionary, particularly for individual investors looking to customize their market exposure. They are cost efficient in terms of fees charged and offer a high level of transparency to the specific stocks and industry sectors targeted by each fund. These attributes will drive continued growth in the popularity of ETFs among both institutional and retail investors, which will result in more new products and strategies being launched and more issuers entering the ETF arena. For you, as an individual investor, the array of choices can make for a lavish, but confusing, smorgasbord.

As you evaluate your choices, it is essential to remember that not all ETFs will attract sufficient interest to survive, no matter how enticing the investment objective or well known the issuer. Consider what has already happened during the past few years. Nearly 300 ETFs joined the market in 2007. The economic realities of 2008, however, revealed that the ETF industry had grown too large and too fast. In 2008, a total of 58 ETFs closed down, many due to poor investor interest. This compares with the first ETF closing, which happened in 2003, a decade after the first fund hit the market. As is still often the case, the first four funds to close were part of a series. Between 2003 and 2007, just one additional ETF closed its doors.

With the ETF market growing again, the same natural selection will come into play, weeding out the weakest and bolstering the strongest. You don't want to place your bets on ETF progeny headed toward extinction. Your aim should be to avoid low-volume funds while benefiting from new copycats that attract volume due to features like lower fees. If you can strike this balance, you will be well positioned to benefit from the growth in the ETF industry. The purpose of this book is to help you reach that objective.

Basic Tenets of ETF Investing

Whatever your investment preference—traditional, passive indexes or those that take a more customized approach—information is power. As a well-informed investor, you must be on the alert for emerging investment themes and sectors that appear well positioned to outperform. As you design a custom portfolio using specific ETFs that meet your objectives, there are certain basic tenets of ETF investing that must be heeded. Three of the most important are: appropriateness, liquidity, and concentration.

Appropriateness

As with all investments, the most important factor to consider before selecting an ETF is appropriateness. ETFs can be used to build core positions, as well as holdings that provide noncorrelated diversity to a portfolio. It is one thing to try to spice up your broad-based portfolio with exposure to a sector you believe will outperform, but it's something else entirely to add too much or to pick the wrong fund altogether. Some ETFs have an extremely narrow scope, which could pose far more risk than an investor is expecting. Choosing a narrowly defined fund on the belief that it will behave like a broader-based ETF would be like mistaking a bowl of jalapenos for spinach; they're both green vegetable products, but that's where the similarity ends.

Appropriateness requires you to think about what you are consuming as an investor. When judging appropriateness, investment objectives and time horizon are two important issues to consider. Are you using ETFs as a long-term investment in your retirement portfolio or are you being more opportunistic in the short term?

When it comes to ETFs, such as those offered by Direxion, Rydex, and ProShares, appropriateness is crucial. Some funds are intended to track their indexes on a daily basis and are not designed for long-term investors. If you decide to use leveraged ETFs—which offer double and triple exposure, short or long, to a particular index—you need to understand the risks involved.

Liquidity

Liquidity is a good measure of investor interest in an ETF product. You can find average daily trading volume numbers on major financial web sites such as Yahoo! Finance. Because ETFs trade in the open market and are affected by forces such as supply and demand, ETFs with higher trading volume tend to be priced closest to what they are actually worth. ETFs such as SPDR (SPY) and Financial Select SPDRs (XLF) see millions of shares trade hands every day. These ETFs are particularly easy to buy and sell, and tend to trade close to their NAVs.

ETFs have two types of liquidity: primary and secondary. Primary liquidity involves the actual liquidity of the fund's underlying basket of securities. In other words, does the fund hold stocks such as Apple and Microsoft that trade millions of shares every day, or does it hold small-cap stocks that are listed on an exchange in Russia? ETFs that have more liquid components would be expected to trade closer to their NAV than funds that have less liquid components.

Secondary liquidity reflects demand for the ETF itself. Are people interested in a particular ETF, or is there a better, more cost-effective alternative? ETFs that can't drum up much volume will tend to trade at a noticeable premium or discount to their NAVs. This secondary effect can also make an impact when a certain sector suddenly gets hot and investors rush into a particular set of ETF products. When the trading volume is increased and there are many more buyers and sellers, you will have more access to liquidity than when that sector is quiet.

Concentration

The third basic tenet of ETF investing is concentration. You must consider two types of concentration risk when adding to your portfolios: product concentration and portfolio concentration. Product concentration refers to dominance of one or a few stocks in an ETF.

If a single stock accounts for 15 percent, 20 percent, or more of an ETF's holdings, that one issue can have a great impact on the success or failure of the fund. If you are looking to mitigate security-specific risk, you should seek out more balanced ETF choices.

More important to consider is the effect that a concentrated ETF can have on your overall portfolio, that is, potentially magnify existing risks. If you already own Microsoft, then adding iShares Dow Jones U.S. Tech (IYW), which in October 2009 had an 11.9 percent allocation in Microsoft, will further accentuate your exposure to that company. Too much concentration can result from ETFs with significant, overlapping positions in a particular stock; for example, one ETF in which Google accounts for 10 percent of the holdings, and another ETF in which Google accounts for 15 percent. As you choose individual ETFs, keep the big picture in mind so as not to have an overconcentration of one issue or another. At all times, it is essential to keep sight of your objectives.

With an understanding of the three basic tenets of ETF investing, it's time to consider the first steps in choosing an ETF. The selection process begins with the description of an ETF's investment purpose, in other words, what the fund intends to do, whether to track a particular index, or to provide exposure to a particular basket of securities. If the investment purpose matches what you are seeking, then this may be a good ETF candidate for your portfolio. But the description only tells part of the story. Not paying attention to the details, such as sector exposure and concentration, would be like buying a house on the basis of the exterior. The façade may look nice, but the interior could be a disaster. In order for you to find a home for your investment dollars, you must consider much more than what the ETF says it will do.

Fund information that is available on most financial information web sites will reveal breakdowns of an ETF's holdings. What are the top securities in its portfolio and what percentage does each represent? What is the amount of concentration in any single stock? How does that impact other holdings in your portfolio? ETFs that track an index such as the Dow Jones Industrial Average have holdings that are spread across several sectors, such as technology, financial, industrials, and so forth. It is possible, however, that an ETF has a more concentrated exposure to a particular sector—whether energy, financial, technology, or another—than its name alone would apply. Unless you are aware of the sector components of each ETF you own, you could end up with a greater exposure to a particular industry than you would otherwise desire.

Other ETF data are also available at a glance; for example, the comparison between the NAV and the price. You would expect a broad-based index with excellent liquidity to have very little difference between its NAV and the price of the ETF. This is not always the case, however, especially with specialized ETFs that prove to be poorly constructed, fail to attract sufficient investor attention, or both.

Active Investing Approach

From funds that offer exposure to broad indexes to those that focus on a particular sector, ETFs are particularly well suited for investors who take an active approach. Before continuing our discussion, let us define what we mean by an active investor. For the purpose of this book, we are *not* defining an active investor on the basis of how many transactions a person makes every week or month. Nor do we mean to encourage a very short-term trading approach with positions that may last only a few days. Rather, we see active investing as encompassing a type of individual who wants to be actively involved in his or her investment decisions. Simply put, you are an active investor if you know what you want—and you are willing to do the necessary homework to target the specific opportunities you wish to pursue.

As an active investor, you are committed to building and managing your portfolio by researching market trends and sector opportunities. Even if you work with a professional advisor, you are continuously engaged, monitoring your portfolios, and ensuring that your investments remain reflective of your goals and objectives. Your mind-set as an active investor is to capture a market trend, seeking to be involved in particular industries and/or sectors as opportunities evolve.

To be an active investor requires that you become well informed—picking the right ETF, staying alert for a change in trend, and watching for the emergence of another opportunity. You know what is in your portfolio and pay special attention to concentration— meaning the overall exposure provided by specific ETFs, as well as the net effect of all ETFs, stocks, and other instruments working in concert. You are informed and empowered as you pursue your specific objectives according to your personal investment time horizons. With this involvement comes a high level of investor accountability. You must be willing to play the role of manager, overseeing portfolios of your own design.

Three Must-Know Types of ETFs

There are many ways that ETFs can pursue their overall goal of tracking their underlying portfolios. For example, an ETF can be made up of 100 different companies in the United States, or it could be made up of companies in other countries, or even hold derivatives. Before you become involved in trading ETFs, you should understand three basic categories of funds.

Domestically Traded Equity ETFs

The first group is domestically traded equity ETFs. All the components of these ETFs are stocks or American Depositary Receipts (ADRs) of foreign stocks that trade on U.S. exchanges. A domestically traded equity ETF and its basket of securities trade within the same regular market hours (9:30 A.M. to 4 P.M. Eastern Time). If there is sufficient investor interest, there will be no deviation between the fund price and the NAV. This group also tends to have lower risk because investments are easily hedgeable, a strategy that we will explore in Chapter 2. Their straightforward nature gives them a complexity rating of beginner—meaning they are fairly easily understood by investors who have some knowledge of ETFs.

Domestically traded equity-based ETFs boast different strategies to expose investors to various sectors or investment themes. A passive indexing strategy will rank all the stocks in a certain category by capitalization or another combination of criteria, and then allocate the fund's assets accordingly. Examples of this kind of ETF include the Financial Select Sector SPDR (XLF), which focuses on companies engaged in investment management and commercial and investment banking; iShares Russell 2000 Index (IWM), which tracks the Russell 2000; and Market Vectors Gold Miners ETF (GDX), which replicates the performance of the NYSE's Arca Gold Miners Index of gold-mining stocks. Even an international-theme ETF that uses domestically traded ADRs—such as PowerShares Golden Dragon Halter USX China Portfolio (PGJ), which is composed of U.S-listed securities of companies that derive a majority of their revenue from the People's Republic of China—is included in this category. If the underlying equity securities trade on U.S. markets, the ETF earns the label of domestically traded equity ETF.

International Equity ETFs

The second group is international equity ETFs, which are a step up on the complexity rating at intermediate to sophisticated. Examples of international equity ETFs include: iShares MSCI Emerging Markets Index (EEM), which invests in companies located in countries such as Brazil, South Korea, Taiwan, China, South Africa, and India, among others; iShares FTSE/Xinhua China 25 Index (FXI), which tracks an index of Chinese companies; and iShares MSCI Germany Index (EWG), which is composed of publicly traded securities in the German market.

As you would expect from the name, securities held by an international equity ETF are not listed on U.S. exchanges. This is an important point to understand. For example, while the ETF itself trades in the United States, the stocks in its underlying basket may be listed on exchanges half the world and numerous time zones away. The discrepancies can cause disconnect between the ETF market price and the underlying fund value. Once the foreign markets where its component securities are closed, the ETF may trade in the United States based on currency movements, what the Dow is doing, or any other number of factors. As a result, the price of the ETF may stray from its NAV, and possibly quite significantly, which often makes it impossible to immediately hedge investments in these funds.

Although many international equity ETFs are large and liquid, as an investor you need to be aware of the complexities of foreign investments, which' can be affected by many factors including currency valuations. International funds may also be impacted by restrictions that result when countries put limitations on foreign investors. For example, Brazil recently imposed a transaction fee on security transactions. While most international equity funds take into account such limitations, you should be watchful for potential unexpected risk that can hit foreign securities, such as in an emerging market. A political situation could quickly put a particular country out of favor for investment. If you hold shares in an ETF that concentrates on that country, when you want to sell your shares you may have to accept a sharply discounted price. Another factor is that many international markets tend to be small, which makes liquidity an issue and affects the pricing of the ETF.

A further consideration with an international cap-weighted ETF is that the top holding could account for a sizeable portion of the portfolio because that particular company accounts for a significant part of the country's overall equity market. Individual country funds may also be very concentrated in terms of sectors because one or a few industries, such as energy or mining, account for most of the country's economy. Keep in mind our main criterion for an ETF: A fund that works is one that tracks its underlying value. If a structural issue with an international fund—such as being narrowly focused or overly weighted toward one equity—causes a discrepancy between the price and the NAV, then that ETF does not work.

Derivative-Based ETFs

The third group of ETFs does not track equities; rather, these funds trade based on a portfolio of derivatives to gain exposure to commodities, currencies, or leveraged strategies. These ETFs are composed of baskets of futures contracts and swaps. The investment objective of these ETFs is to reflect the change in percentage of the spot price of the futures contracts and/or the price of swaps that make up the basket. Because futures and swaps are complex and involve speculation, these ETFs are not for everyone. You should not trade ETFs that hold derivatives unless you understand what you are getting into and the inherent risks involved.

Examples of these types of funds are United States Natural Gas (UNG), which aims to track in percentage terms movements in natural gas prices; United States Oil (USO), which reflects the changes in percentage terms of the spot price of U.S. light sweet crude oil; Direxion Daily Financial Bull 3X Shares (FAS), which seeks to deliver 300 percent of the price performance of the Russell 1000 Financial Services Index using futures and swaps to enhance the trend of the index; and Direxion Daily Financial Bear 3X Shares (FAZ), which has an objective of delivering 300 percent of the inverse (or opposite) of the price performance of the Russell 1000 Financial Services Index and uses futures to replicate a 300 percent short position.

Because these funds are priced off derivatives instead of equities, they are subject to added levels of complexity and risk. Traditionally, derivatives such as futures contracts have been used by producers, whether a wheat farmer or an oil company, to hedge. Speculators have always been part of the derivatives market and contribute to liquidity. Now, however, regulators want to crack down on speculators, as we will discuss in detail later in the book.

These three categories of ETFs illustrate that not all funds are the same. As an investor, you need to know the implications of different types of funds and whether they pose appropriate or excessive risk. In addition, new types of funds are also being introduced. Examples include fixed income, actively managed, and target date ETFs. Target date funds (also known as life-cycle or age-based funds) adjust the ratio between equities and fixed income as a person approaches retirement (the target date). With baby-boomer investors in mind, ETF issuers are launching products such as target date ETFs in hopes of drawing interest from mutual funds. As these types of funds grow in number and popularity, you will gain an advantage by having an understanding of the particular ways in which these funds differ from other types of ETFs.

Expansion in the ETF industry will bring more issuers into the action, which can benefit investors. As more firms join the marketplace, fees will be driven lower. We've already seen proprietary ETFs launched by large financial firms such as Schwab, Vanguard, State

Street, and Fidelity, which in the past have been more closely associated with mutual funds. The aim is to develop a "sticky" customer base that will use the firm for ETFs, mutual funds, financial transactions, and other products. Schwab, for example, recently announced ETFs with no transaction fees for its customers.

No matter what type of ETF you are interested in buying, you must be discerning and not get distracted by a brand name. Becoming more responsible for your investment choices requires you to determine which ETFs are most likely to deliver on their main premise as stated previously: closely tracking an underlying index or portfolio.

The ETF Investor

There is no typical ETF investor. People who use ETFs range in age and have a variety of investment objectives. You can use ETFs to make up for losses in retirement portfolios, or you can trade ETFs in order to pursue greater financial freedom. Your portfolio can be built using funds that track broad indexes, and/or you can focus on sectors that you believe will yield short-term, aggressive growth.

ETFs can be used to realize virtually any investment objective. For example, one client at Dion Money Management has used ETFs to construct a portfolio that meets his number one objective: simplicity at tax time. This objective has governed all his investment decisions, more so than seeking a particular return or trying to opportunistically position himself in industries or market sectors. Over the long term, his return, factoring in dividends, has been consistent with the S&P and Dow.

Granted, not every investor looks to create a portfolio purely on the basis of simplicity at tax time. However, it is a unique example of structuring a portfolio to meet one's individual needs. Other Dion Money Management clients use ETFs for growth, income, capital preservation, and other investment goals, as you will read about throughout the book. Some investors are most interested in broad market exposure using index ETFs, while others may be attracted to ETFs that boast a particular strategy, such as the Vanguard Value ETF

(VTV), which tracks the performance of large-cap value stocks and sounds like a traditional mutual fund.

Others want a high-touch strategy with very narrowly themed ETFs in a customized portfolio. There are also hybrid strategies that combine the two, with a core portfolio that will not change dramatically over time and smaller satellite positions that investors can use to target changes in the marketplace on a shorter time horizon. (And for those investors who do trade ETFs, the tax efficiency of these funds is a positive attribute.) The point is whatever your objective—whether taking a conservative, long-term approach or being more aggressive with short-term moves that target specific sectors—ETFs are the best tools to use.

Portfolio Approach

Investors today are more conscious than ever of wanting and needing an investment approach that is cheaper and more transparent, which adds to the appeal of ETFs. Rather than pay commissions to construct a portfolio stock-by-stock (an exceedingly difficult endeavor, as will be explained in a moment), you can gain exposure to investment themes of your choice through ETFs. More important, there is no need to be a certain-sized investor. Using ETFs you could conceivably gain access to, say, the S&P 500, NASDAQ 100, or a sector such as a biotechnology with as little as one share.

As an active investor, you can use ETFs to gain exposure to a particular sector or market segment without engaging in stock picking. A difficult endeavor even for professionals, consistent stock picking is virtually impossible for the average investor. Even if you successfully identify the overall market trend and you pick the sector that is poised to grow, you can still end up in the wrong stock. A particular issue may be the laggard in its sector for any number of reasons. There are numerous intangibles that can hit a particular stock. A perfect example was the speculation surrounding Apple CEO Steve Jobs, who was noticeably absent from the public eye in early 2009, which fueled rumors about his health as well as corporate succession issues (not to mention the outlook for innovation) at Apple. These concerns sent shockwaves through Apple's share price until Jobs, who had received a liver transplant, returned to the company.

There is another reason why stock picking is often a losing endeavor for so many individual investors. Often by the time investors hear about a hot stock, particularly in the media, that security has already staged a considerable move. A stock that has moved up by a double- or triple-digit percentage may not have much more room to move to the upside. If you buy a stock at that point, you face the very real possibility of being the latecomer who ends up buying at or near the top. This phenomenon is the source of a rule of thumb among professional traders: Look for the odd lots in popular stocks. To explain, stocks typically trade in round numbers in the hundreds or thousands. However, when an odd number of shares such as 201 or 324 trades frequently, that is evidence that individual investors are getting more involved in the stock. Usually, that is a negative indication in the eyes of professional traders that a stock's trend is about to switch to the downside.

The lesson here, which bears repeating, is that your focus as an investor should be on ETFs that will provide exposure to a particular index, industry, or sector—not on finding a stock that you hope will become the next Google.

Conclusion: The Discerning, Active Investor

The dawn of the ETF industry brought transparent, passive indexing strategies that were designed to give investors access to specific sectors at lower fees than mutual funds. As the ETF trend caught on, issuers rapidly expanded their product lines, including with funds that were more specific and narrowly focused. Today, issuers are more conscious than ever of the role that ETFs can play for the larger investor community. As a new swell of ETFs hits the market, pressure is on you, as an investor, to understand what you are getting into and the impact your choices will have on your portfolios.

The proliferation of offerings could make things more difficult as you must now engage in comparison shopping on everything from concentration of holdings to how funds are weighted. The plus side of this process is that fees will become even more reasonable as larger firms compete. You need to be discerning. While ETFs allow access to increasingly exotic strategies, it will be up to you to ask yourself if you should be there in the first place. No matter how broad-based or narrowly focused the ETF, the main factors to consider will be appropriateness, liquidity, and concentration. Whether you want to build a portfolio of longer-term holdings or to trade shorter-term positions to take advantage of an opportunity, the main criterion is to find ETFs that work.

Just because you could make a particular type of investment doesn't mean that you should. There are two sides to every trade, and when it comes to buying and selling ETFs, you need to make sure you have plenty of company. Without sufficient liquidity, there will likely be a significant difference between the price of an ETF and its NAV. Accomplishing your investment goals requires an active mind-set. Commit to becoming more empowered and informed to make the decisions, at the right time and for the right reasons.

Chapter 2

Judging ETFs

Imagine that you're buying a car. When you show up at the dealership, you notice there are rows and rows of the same make and model. A salesperson meets you in the lot, extolling the virtues of this particular vehicle: its fuel efficiency, comfort, and performance. This is a great car, the salesperson promises, patting the hood. And, of course, there is plenty of inventory. All you have to do is put your money down and drive away.

Before you get mesmerized by the sales pitch, you might ask yourself: Is this car the right choice? Sure, the sales pitch makes it sound great, but is it appropriate for you? Do you know anyone who drives this kind of vehicle, someone you can ask about its reliability and maintenance? Come to think of it, have you ever seen anyone driving this car? If not, maybe that's why there are so many models sitting on the lot unsold.

Shopping for an ETF is not all that different. The sales pitch description of a fund may make it sound like the perfect vehicle for your investment dollars. Judging by that alone, you might be temped to park a portion of your portfolio in an ETF without so much as a second thought. However, if you do not carefully consider what is appropriate for you, you could end up with a clunker. Before committing your money, you will want to "check under the hood," examining the components of the fund. Is it made up of liquid domestically traded equities, or does it hold complex securities such as swaps and futures contracts? How concentrated is it among a few or many holdings? What about the liquidity of the fund itself? Is there good trading volume every day?

Taking these factors into consideration will help you to determine whether an ETF will be able to live up to our definition of what makes a good fund, which as you recall from Chapter 1 is one that closely tracks its underlying index. An ETF that trades significantly above or below its net asset value (NAV) is not performing well. There is something fundamentally wrong with the fund, either because of the way it is structured (perhaps the securities it holds are illiquid) or because of external factors such as regulatory trading limits. Whatever the reason, the fund is not efficiently priced, which is a major warning signal for you.

In order to understand how fund pricing works, let's examine how ETFs are created in the first place. This behind-the-scenes look, albeit in simplified form, will help you to gain a better understanding of the correlation between the structure of a fund and its pricing.

Launching a Fund

The genesis of most ETFs follows one of two basic approaches. One is to copy a popular mutual fund theme or existing ETF. In order to gain a following from investors, a copycat fund must have some new twist. In most cases, this means lower fees to attract cost-conscious investors. The other approach is to come up with a new offering in a yet-to-be-claimed niche. With this type of fund, an ETF issuer seeks to become the first in an investment space in order to capture a marketing advantage. Being the first to establish a particular type of ETF is a big deal, as evidenced by the fact that some of the older ETFs, which were the first to be established in a sector, are still the most popular.

As we create our hypothetical ETF, we are going with the latter strategy: establishing a fund with a unique investment purpose—a music ETF. We're even going to give our ETF the catchy symbol of TUNZ. Our objective is to provide investors with the opportunity to gain exposure to companies that generate at least a portion of their revenues and profits from music. Now we have to decide what is going to be in our fund in order to achieve that objective.

After analyzing all the possibilities, we choose four companies whose shares or American Depositary Receipts (ADRs) are traded in the United States. As you recall from Chapter 1, this puts our ETF in the category of domestically traded equity fund. Of course, in the real world, an ETF would have many more holdings. A fund that holds only four stocks would be far too concentrated. For the sake of keeping our example simple, we're going to pretend that wouldn't be a problem. TUNZ holds:

- Sony Corp. ADR (SNE)—The American Depositary Receipts, traded in the United States, of Sony, which is involved a variety of businesses, including the manufacture of CDs, as well as home entertainment production and entertainment products, among many others
- Apple Inc. (AAPL)—The computer and technology giant that makes personal entertainment devices such as iPods
- Warner Music Group (WMG)—A music content company that provides recorded music and music publishing services
- Logitech (LOGI)—A manufacturer of wireless music systems, as well as speakers, headsets, headphones, and earphones, along with other products

Our music ETF could be structured in a few different ways with regard to weighting. It could be weighted based on market capitalization, with the largest company accounting for the biggest portion of the ETF, followed by the second largest, and so forth. Instead, we are going to pursue an equal-weighting strategy, just to keep things simple.

To start, TUNZ will be created with a 50,000-share unit. That means that on the first day of trading, we are going to deliver 12,500 shares each of Sony, Apple, Warner Music, and Logitech. These shares will be delivered, along with any necessary cash or cash equivalents, to an intermediary bank. At that point, with 50,000 shares of the securities in our fund's basket and 50,000 newly created shares of the ETF, both sides are 100 percent hedged.

The way an ETF comes to market is a bit unique and distinct from the process to launch the shares of company that is going public. When a stock begins trading, there is an initial public offering (IPO) of shares that have been priced by the underwriters. ETFs do not have an IPO process. Instead, they are brought to market by authorized participants who act like the stock specialists on the New York Stock Exchange (NYSE). Taking on the role of market makers, the authorized participants have an obligation to make a two-sided market for the ETF, standing ready to continuously buy and sell the product throughout the trading day. In essence, an ETF needs only two parties—the issuer and the market maker—along with a willing exchange to launch a product. The price of the ETF is based on the value of the underlying securities plus a cash component. This makes an ETF rollout vastly easier than an IPO.

Now, let's assume that, from the first day of trading, TUNZ is a hit. Investors are snapping up shares of the ETF, which are sold by the authorized participant. This activity, however, has changed the balance of holdings for the market maker. As you recall, before trading started everything was perfectly matched or hedged. There were 50,000 shares of the ETF and 12,500 shares of each of the four component companies. When the ETF shares sell, the market maker needs to hedge by buying more shares in the underlying portfolio.

Hedging involves trading one thing for something else that is not exactly the same but close. An example we use is you are buying blue and yellow and selling green. With an ETF, the fund shares are the green and the component securities are the blue and yellow. As you can see, your ability to sell green is highly dependent upon the amount of blue and yellow that you can buy. You can't try to substitute extra blue for a shortage of yellow; if you do, it won't be the same green.

Using the TUNZ example, as orders come in, they are filled by the market maker, who is then synthetically short. In order to be hedged again, the authorized participant must buy a corresponding number of the underlying components: Sony, Apple, Warner Music, and Logitech. The market maker faces some risk because of the time gap between selling the ETF shares and going into the market to buy the underlying stocks in order to become hedged again. Compensation for this risk comes in the form of a premium in the price of the ETF. In this example, instead of selling shares of the ETF right in line with the NAV, the market maker charges a small premium—say, two cents a share.

Now let's say that by the time the market maker is able to buy the component stocks, their prices have decreased somewhat. As a result, the NAV is three cents lower than when the ETF shares were sold. The two-cent premium on the ETF selling price and the three-cent drop in the value of the underlying stocks results in a five-cent spread. On the 5,000 shares of the ETF, that translates into a total profit for the market maker of $250. Although that does not sound like much, consider the volume that an actively traded ETF can generate. The average daily trading volume for the Financial Select SPDR ETF (XLF) is well over 100 million shares.

A market maker's profit margin can also be improved by high-speed, high-frequency trading. The authorized participants who are active on the NYSE's Arca all-electronic platform are able to lock in their profits instantly: As soon as ETF shares are sold, the component stocks are bought. Being able to hedge instantaneously eliminates the risk of exposure on either side for the market maker. Not only does this keep the ETF price in line with its NAV, it also translates into a narrow spread between the "bid" (the price at which market makers will buy shares from the investing public) and the "ask" (the price at which market makers will sell their shares to the investing public).

Generally, the spread between the bid and ask can be kept in a tight range as long as there is sufficient liquidity, both in the fund itself and in its component securities. Large, liquid ETFs with portfolios of large companies that are also liquid should be easy to hedge. That translates into a narrow bid–ask spread, which is a sign of efficient pricing and benefits you as the investor. A wide spread, on the other hand, means you will have to buy the shares for more than they are worth and sell them for less than they are worth—hardly the ideal situation. ETFs are different from mutual funds in that they have low fees and trade throughout the day on exchanges. However, a wide spread in an ETF can be as bad as a high fee—and if you can't find someone to trade with, what is the point of buying and selling during the day?

For our TUNZ fund, our goal is to have a narrow spread between the bid and ask prices because we know that is what savvy investors will be looking for. If we've done a good job of structuring the fund so that it can be hedged efficiently, the bid and ask will be in a narrow range.

Now, what happens when we sell all 50,000 shares of the ETF and customers still want more? The authorized participant, who has a bona fide hedging exemption, can continue to sell shares of the ETF, which results in a short position in the underlying stocks. This cannot go on indefinitely. Regulation SHO requires that after 13 consecutive days, a market maker must close out a short position. Within that time frame, a market maker needs to become fully hedged again by buying the component securities. Let's say that demand for TUNZ is so strong that not only have the initial 50,000 shares sold, but another 50,000 as well. Becoming fully hedged again requires the purchase of a corresponding number of shares each of Sony, Apple, Warner Music, and Logitech.

As this simplified example shows, hedging by the authorized participant is critical. If market makers did not stand ready to buy and sell ETFs from the investing public, these funds would trade far from their NAVs, resulting in huge premiums or discounts. This is extremely important to you as an investor. If the portfolio components are difficult to hedge, that ETF will not trade in line with its NAV. An ETF that cannot meet this quality standard is one you should avoid.

A Book Is More than the Proverbial Cover

At this point you might assume that as long as a fund contains large, liquid domestically traded equities, then everything should be fine. A market maker would be able to scoop up big-name stocks in large quantities in order to hedge the ETF shares that are sold. No problem there, right? Let's test that hypothesis. Consider a fund whose top holdings include Exxon Mobil, General Electric, Procter & Gamble,

Chevron, Coca-Cola, and Philip Morris. Moreover, those top holdings range from about 8 percent to a little over 2 percent of the entire
holdings, meaning that the fund is not overly concentrated in any one
issue. Further, the fund has a good spread among the sectors, with oil
and gas accounting for about 30 percent, consumer goods about 25
percent, industries around 22 percent, and utilities about 11 percent,
followed by smaller exposure to basic material, technology, consumer
services, and so forth.

Sounds good, right? On that basis alone, yes, it does sound fine.
Going back to our car-buying analogy, this would be like the salesperson showing you the brochure that extols the virtues of the car.
But just how well has the car sold? What do other consumers have
to say about it? Similarly, when you are buying an ETF, you need
access to the same type of information. Luckily for you, sales data are
available at a glance by looking at just about any financial web site.

Remember the one quality that ETFs all share: transparency.
Everything you need to know is laid out for you; that is, if you are
willing to look for and use the information. In the case of our mystery
ETF, a financial web site in early December 2009 would have revealed
that this particular fund had trading volume for the day of only 1,700
shares. Yes, only 1,700 shares. Compare that to the Financial Select
SPDR, with its average daily volume of 165 million shares. A volume
chart reveals that over the past several months, volume has been very
low, with the exception of a few days when it spiked significantly
higher. That pattern of low volume tells you one important fact:
Other investors have stayed away from this fund. Even though you
may not know the reason immediately, that fact alone should encourage you to do the same.

The mystery fund in our example was the Claymore/Morningstar
Manufacturing Super Sector ETF, which traded under the symbol MZG.
MZG was among four funds that its issuer, Claymore Securities, shut
down in mid-December 2009, along with Claymore/Morningstar Infor-
mation Super Sector Index ETF (MZN), Claymore/Morningstar
Services Super Sector Index ETF (MZO), and Claymore U.S. 1, the
Capital Markets Index ETF (UEM). (See Figures 2.1 and 2.2.)

The question you might be asking is what went wrong with
MZG? It would seem that the fund should have been appealing to

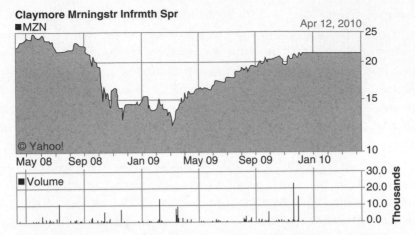

Figure 2.1   MZN shows pattern of low volume of only a few thousand shares a day, except for occasional spikes in trading activity.
SOURCE: Reproduced with permission of Yahoo! Inc. © 2010 Yahoo! Inc. YAHOO! and the YAHOO! logo are registered trademarks of Yahoo! Inc.

investors, given the two strong brand names behind it: issuer Claymore Securities and Morningstar, a very well-respected analysis firm with expertise in indexing. And yet, MZG, which tracked the Morningstar Manufacturing Super Sector Index, failed to attract an investor following. Investors had judged this fund to be unattractive either because it was not unique enough compared with other better-known and

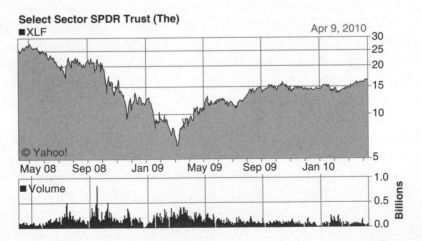

Figure 2.2   By comparison, XLF volume—measured here in billions of shares—is strong, showing excellent liquidity in the fund.
SOURCE: Reproduced with permission of Yahoo! Inc. © 2010 Yahoo! Inc. YAHOO! and the YAHOO! logo are registered trademarks of Yahoo! Inc.

more liquid alternatives, or it was not considered to be a low-cost copycat of other funds.

The MZG example paints a dramatic picture of why you need to research carefully before putting your money down on the basis of a name and a description. There are striking and relevant differences among even seemingly straightforward funds that offer exposure to an index of large-cap, highly liquid equities that trade in the United States. Just because a fund invests in liquid securities doesn't mean the ETF itself will have liquidity. As you recall from Chapter 1, there are two types of liquidity—primary and secondary—and an ETF must have both.

Primary liquidity refers to the liquidity of the securities held by the fund. Clearly MZG did not have an issue with primary liquidity. There is no shortage of shares in companies such as Exxon, General Electric, and Procter & Gamble. Secondary liquidity, however, refers to the liquidity of the fund itself. For whatever reason, MZG failed to attract sufficient investor interest long before the fund announced it was shutting down. MZG was a zombie, an investment creature that you want to avoid.

Beware of Zombies

For every fund that captures high liquidity and changes hands millions of times a day, such as the SPDR S&P 500 (SPY) and PowerShares QQQ (QQQQ), there are many low-liquidity funds with little trading volume and unacceptably large spreads. In a free market, however, you can't force people to buy and sell shares of your fund. No matter how appealing an ETF might be—because it's well constructed, follows a sensible approach, or targets an appealing strategy—you can't just make liquidity happen. The ETF industry is driven by consumer demand, and investors have to want the fund.

If there are plenty of buyers and sellers, then a fund is easy to hedge, giving the market maker a tremendous opportunity for arbitrage. The market maker reaps a profit, thanks to strong investor demand, which in turn keeps the bid-ask spread narrow and helps to attract even more investors, and so the cycle continues.

When a well-intentioned fund comes to market but fails to attract a following, it may limp along for a while. Eventually, unless trading steps up, the fund could join the ranks of the undead—ETFs that haven't been put out of their misery, but do not have much life either. It will become a zombie fund.

The problem with zombie funds goes right back to the explosion of the ETF industry itself. As the newest investing ideas took shape, ETF issuers rushed to develop products that match the trend. Although ETF launches reflect investor demand, they are often slightly behind the curve. The process by which a market maker gives capital to an issuer is called seeding. In the past, this has been helpful, enabling issuers to launch five or six funds at a time in hopes that even one of the funds would be profitable from a trading perspective. Overall, this has been a very good thing: More choices of funds that target various strategies, with transparency that allows you to see what the fund holds, how it is priced, and how much volume it is attracting. The explosion in popularity of ETFs has encouraged issuers to pump out even more products to get a piece of the action. In the heyday of launches, ETF issuers would sometimes introduce as many as 10 products in a single day, knowing that the popularity of a few could sustain a whole line.

In the third quarter of 2009 alone, there were more than 500 ETFs slated for release. As we noted earlier, companies like Schwab have joined the ETF race, which will probably inspire even more asset managers to start up their own lines. So what's the problem? ETF issuers will overshoot and overproduce, with more products in the marketplace than are sustainable. In 2008, 58 ETFs were shuttered, and as of late August 2009, another 45 closed down. As more and more funds come out, not all of them will be profitable. Investors must be aware of the potential for a fund to turn into a zombie that lacks the life-blood of liquidity. Any fund that fails to generate liquidity and cannot trade near its NAV is defeating the whole purpose of what an ETF is supposed to be.

When a fund lacks investor interest, it can be shut down. Notice is given to investors by the issuer that, in return for their shares, they will get the value of the fund. The good news, therefore, is that the fund will not go to zero, unlike a stock that is getting delisted. For the ETF investor, this presents a choice: Sell your shares immediately, which may mean taking a pounding because everyone else is bailing out, or you can take the risk and wait. When you get stuck in an ETF as it winds down, your money is tied up. Your opportunity cost is being unable to reinvest your capital elsewhere—to say nothing of the uncertainty of whether the NAV is going to rise or fall. The dangers of a zombie fund provide ample warning as to why investors should stay away from illiquid funds.

Illiquidity puts an unnecessary strain on investors. The problem will never be on the buy side, since many issuers promote liquidity. Because ETFs want to get bigger, market makers are encouraged to create new shares at a pace of 50,000 or 100,000 at a pop. The problem for the investor is when it is time to sell 100 or 500 of their ETF shares in the open market.

Creation and redemption happen daily in large and highly liquid funds. In illiquid funds, creation will happen at the fund's conception, and perhaps stop entirely. When you invest in an ETF, you want to have lots of company. To use the car analogy again, when you buy that spiffy roadster, you want to see them everywhere. If you are out there alone in your ETF, when it comes time to sell, you could find yourself trapped in a zombie nightmare.

Nontraditional ETFs

Our discussion thus far has illustrated the importance of liquidity, especially to avoid thinly traded funds. But what about a fund that trades millions of shares a day? What could be the problem here? The answer depends upon what the fund holds in its basket of securities.

The first ETFs were introduced as passive, low-cost, and transparent vehicles. Now, there are nontraditional ETFs that utilize a host of indexing approaches. Nontraditional funds such as Direxion Daily Financial Bull 3X (FAS), U.S. Natural Gas (UNG), and iPath India (INP) have drawn a considerable amount of investor attention—meaning they have good secondary liquidity. However, they are cloaked in complexity, which makes these funds best left to experienced, sophisticated investors.

One type of nontraditional fund is the leveraged ETF, which uses futures or swaps as part of its indexing strategies, thus promising investors the chance to double or triple their exposure. For example, Direxion Daily Financial Bull 3X (FAS) seeks daily investment results that are 300 percent of the price performance of the Financial Select Sector Index. Similarly, the ProShares Ultra Financials (UYG) aims to produce daily investment results that correspond to 200 percent of the daily performance of the Dow Jones U.S. Financials Index. While these funds may be useful for sophisticated traders who are hedging a larger strategy, they are inappropriate for long-term investors. These funds use a daily resetting technique that, combined with volatility, can erode the ETFs over time.

Similar problems exist in inverse funds that seek to perform the opposite of the index that they track. For example, ProShares UltraShort Financial (SKF) seeks daily investment results, before fees and expenses, that are 200 percent the inverse or opposite of the daily performance of the Dow Jones U.S. Financial Index. If the financial index declines by, say, 10 percent, the SKF would seek to have a 20 percent gain. Inverse funds, however, use futures to replicate a short position. Not only do derivatives in a portfolio make for complex pricing and hedging, but intervention by regulators can impact the normal operation of a fund.

Consider what happened in 2008, when in the midst of the financial crisis, investors rushed to short-sell financial stocks. Regulators became concerned that the short-selling was threatening firms such as Citigroup and Bank of America, which were under pressure. As a result, regulators banned short-selling in some financial stocks. For traders who wanted a short position, the only alternative was to buy shares in an ETF such as SKF.

The regulatory agencies picked up on the trading volume and tried to stem the flow of money into these inverse ETFs that were perceived as contributing to the downward pressure in the market. Therefore, agencies said that no additional units of SKF could be created. When market makers can't create additional units, funds trade wildly away from their NAVs. Then, traders have to increase their spreads to compensate for being unable to hedge.

Concern over leveraged and inverse funds has prompted the Financial Industry Regulatory Authority (FINRA), the largest independent regulator for all securities firms that do business in the United States, to issue an alert. FINRA warned individual investors about leveraged and inverse funds, urging caution and more education for those who may not understand how these funds work.

For all these reasons we hesitate to talk about leveraged funds, other than to note that, when used appropriately by professional traders, they can be effective tools to hedge intraday; for example, buying a leveraged ETF at 9:30 Eastern in the morning and selling it at 11:30, and then buying a position again at 1:00 in the afternoon and selling it before the market closes at 4:00. Leveraged funds have a daily trading objective and are for professionals only. Anyone else should stay away.

Another type of nontraditional ETF is a futures-based commodity ETF, which invests in baskets of futures or swaps. Unlike equities, however, futures contracts expire. Therefore, in order to keep the fund going, market makers have to sell the contracts that are expiring and buy more. That added complexity causes disparity between the price of the fund and the price of the portfolio that it is supposed to track. When the roll date occurs (when a position in expiring contracts must be rolled into the next month), the result can also be a premium or discount to the NAV. The disconnect goes to the heart of the fund's effectiveness to track its underlying index. By our definition of what makes a good fund, this would not be an appropriate choice for investors.

There is another complication that can occur with ETFs holding futures in their portfolios: contango, which is based upon the relationship between the price of a futures contract and the spot price of a commodity in the future. With contango, the futures price starts above the spot price and then falls over time as the two align. For example, a futures contract that is priced at $90 today decreases in value to $80. (The opposite of contango is backwardation, with the futures price below the spot price in the future. The futures price must increase over time, so what is worth $90 today rises to $100.)

Contango, however, can be a major problem for commodity speculators, including an ETF that holds these instruments. United States Natural Gas ETF (UNG) had a problem with contango for most of 2009, when the price of natural gas futures in the front month was higher than those with later deliver dates. UNG only buys front-month futures contracts, which it must sell as they near expiration. With prices in contango, the fund had to sell futures at falling prices and buy more expensive contracts one month out.

Natural gas prices were not the only worry for UNG (see figure 2.3). In June 2009, investors began buying shares of the fund at a fast pace. As the fund became more popular, more and more natural gas futures contracts had to be purchased in order to create more ETF shares. This activity in the futures market caught the eyes of regulatory authorities, in particular the Commodity Futures Trading Commission (CFTC), which was concerned that instead of tracking the natural gas futures market, UNG was influencing it. When the tail wags the dog, regulators are not happy.

With the CFTC considering new position limits even for bona fide hedgers such as ETF market makers, UNG temporarily halted the creation of new shares in July 2009. By late September, UNG had resumed issuance of shares. However, position limits imposed by the CFTC could impact the fund in the future. If that happens, the pricing mechanism will be knocked for a loop.

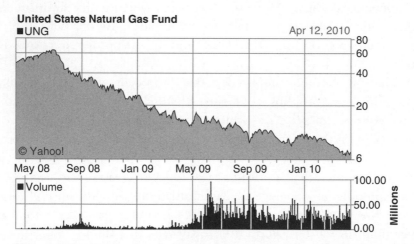

Figure 2.3 Fund prices for UNG have been under pressure due to falling natural gas prices. UNG also faces regulatory limits on how many futures contracts a fund can hold.
SOURCE: Reproduced with permission of Yahoo! Inc. © 2010 Yahoo! Inc. YAHOO! and the YAHOO! logo are registered trademarks of Yahoo! Inc.

There are other nontraditional ETFs such as exchange-traded notes (ETN) that, instead of holding baskets of equities, invest in a debt portfolio—specifically unsubordinated debt notes (which is what the "N" in ETN stands for). When ETNs were first introduced in 2006, investors rushed to put their money in these instruments that were proclaimed to be the newest and hottest thing in exchange-traded products. Three years later, ETNs are contracting. According to data from the National Stock Exchange, the total number of listed ETNs decreased from 90 in October 2009 to 84 in October 2009.

As the ETF industry continues to expand, expect other varieties of funds to appear in the future. In order to judge which funds are most appropriate, investors cannot rely only on what the issuer promises any more than you would listen solely to a salesperson at the car dealership (and particularly one with a lot full of unsold inventory). Performance is where the rubber meets the road. That doesn't mean that investors should back away from ETFs altogether. ETFs are revolutionary products that can help investors achieve their investment goals. However, there are some types of funds that are inappropriate because of their complexity and pricing. The only way investors can make that determination is to become empowered with education and information.

Keep Your Eyes Open

With regulators increasing their scrutiny of funds, it is no surprise that fund issuers have stepped up their disclosure and have even taken such dramatic steps at times as halting creation of new shares and stopping sales. Investors, too, have to do their part. With an understanding of how ETFs are created and priced, as we have discussed in this chapter, investors can see why some funds have narrow spreads and some do not; why some are able to track their underlying index while others cannot. That is the purpose of this book: to educate investors, particularly those who choose to become active in ETF trading.

The age of investor ignorance is over. The ETF universe provides ample choices for long-term allocation, along with the potential to take advantage of opportunities in sectors and subsectors on a shorter-term basis. Regulations may help to differentiate between ETFs that are appropriate for investors and those that are inappropriate for anyone but the most experienced and sophisticated. Until that happens, investors need to err on the side of caution when selecting ETFs.

Let's review the type of information you need as part of your process to determine whether an ETF is appropriate for you. Here is a simple, step-by-step plan that can help you access readily available information to judge whether an ETF is appropriate for you.

- Name of the fund and the symbol. In order to access information about the fund on a financial web site such as Yahoo! Finance, you will need the trading symbol or "ticker" of the fund.
- Look at the three-month average trading volume of the fund. Most financial web sites will allow you to see a volume number for the most recent trading day as well as the average volume over a three-month period. The bigger the volume, the better the secondary liquidity, meaning the demand in the marketplace for the ETF shares from investors.
- What is the amount of total assets?
- What is the expense ratio?
- What are the top 10 holdings in the fund, and what percentage of the portfolio do they represent? Is the fund overly concentrated in a few stocks?

With an understanding of pricing and trading, you can look at the layers of liquidity involved. Does the fund hold liquid securities, or does it invest in instruments that are complex or thinly traded? What about the liquidity of the fund itself? Is there good average trading volume measuring in millions of shares every day, which indicates a strong investor following, or is there little trading volume in only thousands of shares?

Based on just these few factors alone, you should be able to make a pretty good decision about the appropriateness of an ETF, and compare one ETF to another. With these transparent instruments, the information is there for you to access. It's up to you to use it.

Chapter 3

Understanding Indexing: New Options for Investors

T he ETF industry has come a long way from its plain vanilla days when funds only tracked passive indexes. Today, there is a wider assortment of flavors, from interesting to exotic, offered to meet the tastes of just about any investor. As you consider the array of choices, you need to decide which of these funds are pleasing to your palate, given your goals, time horizon, and investment needs.

At one end of the table are the traditional passively indexed ETFs, such as the SPDR Dow Jones Industrial Average (formerly known as the DIAMOND Trust) (DIA), which tracks the Dow Jones Industrial Average. These funds seek to track closely their underlying benchmarks, a strategy that makes them consistent and transparent. In other words, with these funds you know exactly what you're getting. At the other end are actively managed funds, a kind of fusion cuisine between fund manager expertise and the basic structure of an ETF. The problem, however, is that actively managed ETFs lack the transparency of their more traditional counterparts. That is something to keep in mind as you judge whether an actively managed ETF is appetizing to you.

Between the two extremes of passively indexed and actively managed funds is an assortment of choices. For example, there are funds that take a customized approach, starting with a traditional index such as S&P 500, and then spicing it up by ranking stocks according to revenue. Admittedly, all this variety does add to the complexity of the ETFs industry. You may be tempted to stick only with what you know, the traditional passively indexed ETFs, or you may be tempted to sample funds on the basis of a brand name alone. Without full knowledge of the ingredients of a fund (whether it holds domestic or international equities, currencies, or derivatives) and the recipe for putting it together, you could end up with a case of investment heartburn.

Traditional ETFs

As we begin our discussion, let's start with the basics: passively indexed ETFs that track traditional indexes. These were the first offerings from the ETF industry dating back, as mentioned in Chapter 1, to 1993 with the SPDR S&P 500 (SPY) or "spider," as it is called. Fund companies picked an index such as the Dow or the Russell 2000 and created funds that closely track them. The purpose of these ETFs was to offer investors a lower-cost alternative to indexed mutual funds. Most of the passive indexes (but not all) are weighted according to market capitalization so that the company with the largest market capitalization is the biggest component of the index, followed by the stock with the second largest market cap, and so on. ETFs that track these indexes are constructed in the same way and are skewed toward the largest firms.

As an investor, you can reap several advantages from traditional passively indexed ETFs. For one, they are extremely transparent. When you buy one of these funds, you know exactly what you are getting and why. For example, the S&P 500 (which is not market cap–weighted, contrary to popular belief) contains the 500 leading and most widely held companies across several industries. As of January

2010, the top holdings in the index were Exxon Mobil, Microsoft, Procter & Gamble, Apple, Johnson & Johnson, and General Electric. Is it any wonder that the SPY has the exact same holdings? No, not at all, because the purpose of a passively indexed ETF is to track an index—not to beat it or to add any other spin on the ball.

Passively indexed ETFs provide broad-market exposure in an easy and cost-efficient manner. Investing in these ETFs is certainly more appealing than trying to do it on your own by building a port-folio of individual stocks that would have to be weighted in a certain way, which would be a very expensive and onerous process. Although they are the plain vanilla among fund offerings, these ETFs are extremely popular. If all you want to do is gain exposure to a broad market index, why not choose an investment vehicle that is the cheap-est and most efficient way to accomplish that goal? No wonder passively indexed ETFs remain the bread and butter of the industry (see Figure 3.1).

Passively indexed ETFs also carry an advantage for large, profes-sional traders who want to hedge their positions. Let's say that a proprietary trader with several positions is short the overall market.

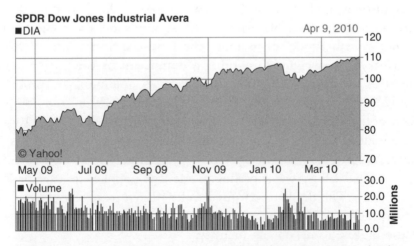

Figure 3.1 The SPDR Dow Jones Industrial Average (DIA) closely tracks the Dow Jones Industrial Average and trades in the millions— and sometimes tens of millions—of shares each day.

Source: Reproduced with permission of Yahoo! Inc. © 2010 Yahoo! Inc. YAHOO! and the YAHOO! logo are registered trademarks of Yahoo! Inc.

Buying an indexed ETF that mimics the broad market allows a trader to hedge his or her positions quickly and efficiently. Although this type of activity is not recommended for the average retail investor, it does illustrate the wide appeal of ETFs that closely track the major indexes.

As popular as passively indexed ETFs are, they do have a downside. Even though they are constructed exactly like the indexes they are tracking, these ETFs will never allow you to reap the exact same return as their underlying benchmarks, let alone beat them. The reason is you must pay the expenses associated with the funds (albeit lower fees than those charged for a comparable mutual fund), as well as brokerage commissions, which means your return will automatically lag the index. Nonetheless, if your investment goal for all or part of your portfolio is to gain exposure to the broad market in a transparent and cost-efficient manner, passively indexed ETFs offer a viable way to accomplish that.

Targeting Sectors with Cap-Weighted Indexes

In addition to ETFs that track the major indexes, there are other funds that target specific sectors. Many of these funds are also weighted by market-capitalization. For example, the Financial Sector SPDR (XLF) is a market cap–weighted fund that is dominated by the biggest companies in the financial sector. Looking at its holdings, you probably wouldn't be surprised to see that as of January 2010 the top components of the fund are JPMorgan Chase, Bank of America, Wells Fargo, and Goldman Sachs. If you wanted exposure to these big names in the financial sector, the transparency of a market cap–weighted ETF such as the XLF is very appealing. Same thing applies to a sector like technology: The SPDR Tech fund (XLK) listed its top holdings as of January 2010 as Microsoft, Apple, IBM, AT&T, and Google—some of the biggest names in the industry.

With a market cap–weighted sector ETF, the methodology is understandable and accessible. There is no need for you to guess; you know exactly how stocks are picked and how they are weighted. The predictability of these cap-weighted sector funds is a definite plus for you. In order for your trading strategy to work, the funds you pick must be stable and consistent in their approach.

As with any investment vehicle, there are always drawbacks, and market cap–weighted sector funds have their disadvantages, too. Let's take the example of PowerShares QQQ Trust (QQQQ). Although this ETF is considered to be broad-based, it tracks the NASDAQ 100, which is a market cap–weighted index that heavily favors technology. It's no surprise then that the top holdings in QQQQ are large-cap technology companies, including (as of January 2010) Apple, Qualcomm, Microsoft, Google, and Cisco Systems.

As we've seen in the past, there are times when companies such as technology firms trade at prices that are not reflective of their fundamental value. Think about what happened with Internet companies during the dot-com boom of the late 1990s and early 2000 when stock prices were inflated by speculative interest. (They didn't call it the Internet bubble for nothing.) When a particular stock is trading above its fundamental value, its market cap is also inflated. With market cap weighting, a higher price will dictate that stock's percentage in a portfolio. Therefore, you may end up with a sector ETF whose top holding, accounting for 10 percent or more of the fund, is a stock with a price that has been propelled higher by speculation.

In a perfect world, supply and demand would be in equilibrium and the resulting stock price would reflect the fundamentals of the company. The reality, however, is there are anomalies, or outliers, that occur because of perception (and a good dose of fear and greed). In these instances, there is a total disconnect between the price of a stock and what it is really worth. With a market cap–weighted passive index there is no other choice. Regardless of what is moving a stock price, if a company has a large market capitalization, it will account for a greater percentage of the ETF.

Many people also argue that market cap–weighted indexes ignore valuable smaller cap firms whose stock prices do not reflect their real value or potential. These firms may be hampered by a cyclical setback or another factor that has dragged them down. Although these stocks may be attractive from an investment standpoint, their depressed prices keep them underweighted in a cap-weighted index. Eventually, market equilibrium will prevail. When a fund rebalances its holdings, typically a quarterly occurrence, then a more realistic valuation and market cap will be applied. Despite these idiosyncrasies, cap-weighted ETFs do provide exposure to specific market sectors in a logical, understandable, and transparent way.

Beating the Market with Customized Index ETFs

The first generation of ETF investors came to expect funds that are totally passive and transparent, with an objective of closely tracking an index. With passive indexes, investors understood the advantages offered by ETFs of lower fees, greater transparency, and intraday trading. However, as we have discussed, there are also disadvantages, such as never being able to beat an index, that have become real setbacks for ETFs. In the past, if investors wanted to beat a particular benchmark, their only choice was to continue to rely on mutual fund managers.

Today, ETF issuers have responded to the needs of investors who want more from a fund than just passive indexing. Issuers are offering a variety of choices in ETFs, including funds that seek to beat their benchmarks by using specific value-added investment strategies. As a result, these new types of ETFs are gaining in familiarity and popularity among many investors.

The potential market for these types of funds is huge. Consider the $1 trillion retirement savings market that has been dominated by mutual funds. The largest investment demographic today is composed of baby-boomer investors who are looking to build (or rebuild, as the case may be after the steep stock market downturn) their financial nest eggs for the future. Baby boomers are all about choice and doing things their way. ETF issuers are now seeing potential that they have not pursued before—that is, until now. With customized index products, ETFs are poised to capture even more investor interest.

We should state up front that once you get away from traditional market cap weighting and start walking the path toward active management, the ways in which index strategies work become less obvious. Some methodologies are not as intuitive as stating that the top five holdings in the fund will be the top five companies in an index or sector based upon market capitalization. That being said, information about the holdings in the fund will be readily available to you. However, you have to do your homework to understand how the components in an underlying index or portfolio are chosen based upon specific selection criteria or methodology.

A customized index ETF offers a new way to interpret traditional indexes. Instead of creating indexes based only on market capitalization, customized indexes use different criteria such as revenues. Whatever the factors for selecting and weighting stocks, they should be measurable and based on some logical rationale. Let's take a hypothetical example: the Dion Financial ETF. Instead of being a market cap-weighted ETF in the financial sector, such as the Financial Sector SPDR (XLF), the Dion Financial ETF would use a modified market capitalization weighting strategy that also takes into account dividends and earnings, and rebalances its holdings once a year. The stocks in the Dion Financial ETF may be similar to those in a traditional sector fund such as the XLF, but the exact composition and weighting is different because of selection criteria that go beyond market capitalization.

The main point for you to grasp with this hypothetical example is that funds using customized indexing are not merely a mirror of traditional passive indexes. Rather, fund issuers create new indexes or put unique spins on existing indexes by employing other selection criteria such as dividends, earnings, or return on investment. Although funds that use this type of investment rationale do involve some creativity, the result is nearly the same level of transparency as you would have with a passive index. You can easily see what components are in the ETF at any particular point in time and understand how the fund issuer chose and weighted them. Whether or not a particular weighting strategy is appealing will be strictly up to you. Nonetheless, customized index ETFs have the potential (although obviously there is no guarantee) of beating the underlying benchmark.

For example, WisdomTree takes a value approach with its customized ETFs. As WisdomTree states on its web site, it sees a benefit to measuring a company's value using indicators such as dividends and earnings, not stock price alone. WisdomTree has numerous ETFs under several investment themes: U.S. equity-earnings and U.S.

equity-dividends ETFs; and fixed income, international, and currency ETFs. A criticism of the WisdomTree approach is that its value-based criteria exclude many growth opportunities. For example, its selection for dividends would rule out many companies in sectors such as biotechnology and technology that do not pay dividends the way that industrial, utility, and consumer products companies do. Also keep in mind that in the midst of the crisis of 2008, many financial companies, including some with healthy balance sheets, were forced to slash their dividends.

Similarly, screening for earnings would exclude many biotech and technology companies that have much promise, but lack profits currently. Consider Amazon (AMZN), which was a great stock for a long time before it generated earnings. With a value approach that emphasizes earnings, however, Amazon would not have been considered as an index candidate until it generated a profit.

Let's look at another example of a customized approach: RevenueShares ETFs. RevenueShares does not try to completely recreate the wheel by devising an index; instead it constructs funds based on S&P indexes. Then RevenueShares applies its revenue criteria to the stocks that have been selected by S&P. RevenueShares believes that ranking stocks by revenue can produce attractive returns because, as it states on its web site, revenue "resists bias and manipulation." Take its RevenueShares Large Cap Fund (RWL), which is composed of the same stocks that are in the S&P 500 and are then weighted on the basis of revenue. The top holdings in the RevenueShares Large Cap Fund as of January 2010 were Wal-Mart, Exxon Mobil, General Electric, Chevron, and Bank of America. Compare this with the S&P lineup at the time of Exxon Mobil, Microsoft, Apple, Procter & Gamble, and Johnson & Johnson.

Revenue is an interesting criterion because all companies have it, including those that do not have profits as yet, just like all publicly traded companies have market capitalization. The revenue-weighted approach, although nontraditional, still produces a very transparent way to modify an existing index. We would expect to see other well-known indexes receiving a similar customized treatment in the future as more fund issuers seek not only to track their benchmarks, but also to beat them.

As you can see, customized indexing is one step down the path toward active management. The fund issuer chooses some stocks and excludes others based on specific criteria. If you are a true disciple of passive indexing, this will never do! However, if you are looking for a customized approach to help you beat an index, these funds might be good candidates for you to consider.

Dynamic ETFs

Farther down the road toward active management are the dynamic ETFs, which do more than weight stocks in an existing index on the basis of a factor such as revenue. Dynamic ETFs seek to establish unique indexes based on a variety of selection criteria. Consider the PowerShares Dynamic funds, which cover large-cap, small-cap, and mid-cap portfolios, as well as several sectors. PowerShares Dynamic funds utilize multiple screens to select and weight stocks in their indexes. For example, the PowerShares Dynamic Biotechnology & Genome Portfolio (PBE) selects stocks based on an "investment merit criteria," which includes fundamental growth, stock valuation, investment timeliness, and risk factors.

With a dynamic ETF, the objective is to outperform a benchmark such as the S&P 500 or the Russell 2000—or, as they say in investment lingo, to generate "alpha." The problem, however, is one of transparency. Although the fund holdings are disclosed by the ETF, at the end of the day the question becomes whether investors really do understand what they are getting. With an ETF that tracks a passive index such as the S&P 500, there can be no doubt in your mind. Even with a customized approach, things are still pretty transparent because weighting is based on one or only a few criteria.

With a dynamic approach, the selection criteria become more complex. Consider the First Trust AlphaDex ETFs, which employ what First Trust calls "enhanced indexing" in order to pursue alpha. The First Trust AlphaDEX funds start with a traditional index. Then a series of "fundamental screens and factors" are used to rank the stocks in an "enhanced index." For example, the First Trust Large Cap Core AlphaDEX Fund (FEX) is based upon the S&P 500 Index, to which a proprietary stock selection methodology is applied, including growth factors such as 3-, 6-, and 12-month price appreciation, sales to price, and one-year sales growth, as well as value factors such as book value to price, cash flow to price, and return on assets. After all the criteria are applied, each stock is scored. The bottom 25 percent are eliminated and the top 75 percent are selected for the Defined Large Cap Core index. Next, the stocks are divided into quintiles based on their scores. The top-rated quintiles receive greater weight within the index, which is reconstituted and rebalanced quarterly.

First Trust AlphaDEX says that its enhanced indexing is "inherently passive" because no "active judgment' is made when evaluating stocks, and every step in its indexing process is transparent and repeatable. We beg to differ. Once a fund issuer starts applying multiple screens, things are not so straightforward anymore. More subjectivity is involved to determine the factors by which the stocks are evaluated, selected, and weighted.

Nonetheless, if these actively managed funds do outperform a passive index, they will be attractive to investors. After all, performance does matter, particularly the ability to beat a benchmark. One caveat to keep in mind is benchmark-beating performance and the services of a fund company to construct a customized portfolio will come at a price—higher fees for investors.

To summarize our discussion thus far, growth in the ETF industry has resulted not only in a larger number of funds, but also a greater variety. There are the traditional passively indexed ETFs, most of which are market cap-weighted. Although highly popular and widely held, these funds will always be relegated to trailing their underlying indexes, no matter how closely they track them. Next, there are the customized indexes that may seek to tweak an existing index on the basis of factors such as revenue or dividends. Finally, there are dynamic funds that use a variety of selection criteria or screens to choose and weight the stocks.

Next, let's take a look at funds that break the traditional ETF mold with proprietary criteria for constructing an index, as well as actively managed funds that are based largely on the expertise of the manager.

Life-Cycle and Hedge Fund ETFs

There are new ETF offerings in the market today that are marketed on the basis of their ability to deliver a specific outcome. Among these funds are life-cycle ETFs and hedge fund ETFs. Life-cycle ETFs are being marketed heavily to baby boomers for their retirement portfolios. These funds offer automatic asset allocation that follows along a life cycle: more aggressive in the beginning and more conservative at the end, as the investor presumably is nearing retirement. There is no need for you to do any asset allocation yourself; the fund does it all. All you have to do is pick the right retirement target date—and, of course, the right fund. For example, life-cycle funds include several under the TDAX Independence brand, with target dates over a 30-year span, as of this writing out to 2040.

Thus far, life-cyle ETFs have not caught on, although that might possibly be explained by their debut in 2007–2008, which was hardly a great time for the stock market. Despite the slow start for life-cycle ETFs, this is not the last that we'll see or hear from them. The promise of the $1 trillion retirement industry is too great for the ETF industry to pass up. However, there are some drawbacks that might limit the potential of these funds.

The implied presumption is that investors will commit their money and walk away to let the fund do its work over the long term. However, for active investors, the hands-off approach doesn't cut it. In fact, that laissez-faire attitude seems incompatible with an investment product that trades all day, which is one of the major premises of an ETF in the first place. And be honest: What are the chances that you wouldn't look at your life-cycle ETF on a regular basis even though the full benefit of the fund can only be realized over the long term? The problem is this approach makes a life-cycle ETF an island unto itself in a sea of more actively traded products.

Perhaps this helps to explain why life-cycle funds have had comparatively lower volume than their counterparts that appeal to active investors and traders. For example, The TDX Independence 2030 ETF (TDN) trades only in the *thousands* of shares per day, as Figure 3.2 shows.

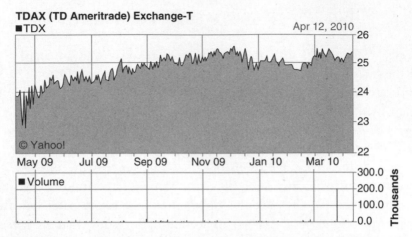

Figure 3.2 TDX Independence 2030 ETF, a life-cycle fund, has volume in the thousands of shares, compared to millions of shares daily in traditional passively indexed funds.
SOURCE: Reproduced with permission of Yahoo! Inc. © 2010 Yahoo! Inc. YAHOO! and the YAHOO! logo are registered trademarks of Yahoo! Inc.

If you do invest in a life-cycle ETF, you have to understand the basic strategy that over time you're going to go from being aggressively invested to being conservatively invested, culminating with a target date that is supposed to coincide with when you retire. If you are going to get involved in this type of ETF, you have to know the game plan and let the fund run its course.

Also in the "island unto itself" category are hedge fund ETFs. IndexIQ, for example, has developed ETFs that seek to replicate hedge fund strategies to capture the risk and return performance of hedge fund investment styles. For example, its IQ Hedge Multi-Strategy Tracker ETF (QAI) tracks a proprietary index that seeks to replicate the risk-adjusted return of hedge funds using strategies such as long/short equity, global macro, market neutral, event-driven, fixed income arbitrage, and emerging markets.

Clearly the opportunity that's being exploited here is offering a hedge fund–type investment to the average investor through a product with shares that trade in the open market. Similar to the life-cycle fund, the hedge fund ETF requires time for its strategy to show what it can do. This is not the kind of fund you want to buy on a

Figure 3.3 Volume for the IQ Hedge Multi-Strategy Tracker ETF (QAI) measures in the tens of thousands of shares
SOURCE: Reproduced with permission of Yahoo! Inc. © 2010 Yahoo! Inc. YAHOO! and the YAHOO! logo are registered trademarks of Yahoo! Inc.

Wednesday and sell on a Friday. Much like the life-cycle product, the hedge fund ETF requires a degree of faith on your part that a fund can execute its strategy. This may explain why hedge fund ETFs also see lighter volume than their more traditional ETF brethren, as Figure 3.3 illustrates.

Currency Carry Trade ETFs

Another twist on indexing is the currency carry trade fund, which has become popular with retail investors looking to take advantage of relationships between currencies. Rather than engage in a complex currency carry trade—which seeks to capture the movement of two currencies, for example, short the U.S. dollar and long Japanese yen (or vice versa)—you can buy a fund that replicates that exposure. Consider the PowerShares DB G10 Currency Harvest Fund (DBV), which seeks to profit from movements in certain G10 currencies. The premise, according to the fund, is that "currencies associated with relatively high interest rates, on average, tend to rise in value relative to currencies associated with relatively low interest rates." Once again, one of the components in the strategy is time. If the yen is going to depreciate and the dollar is going to strengthen, it will happen over a period of time. (Currency ETFs are also discussed in Chapter 8.)

Like more traditional funds, these cutting-edge ETFs—life-cycle, hedge fund, and currency carry trade—all have an underlying index. However, these indexes have been created specifically to mimic a particular strategy. This is far different than tracking a passive index such as the Dow Jones Industrial Average or the Russell 2000, or trying to beat a benchmark with a customized spin on an existing index. Thus, no matter how much the creators of these innovative funds claim they are passive, that is not true in the classic sense. Life-cycle, hedge fund, and currency carry trade ETFs are far closer to actively managed funds than any products we have discussed thus far.

Now it's time to look at actively managed ETFs and how fund issuers are positioning these new products in the market.

Active ETFs

The next group of funds that we are going to discuss is a complete break from the pack: actively managed ETFs. These funds do not track an index. Rather, a fund follows a portfolio that is constructed on the basis of a fund manager's investment hypothesis. Therefore, when you invest in one of these actively managed ETFs, what you're buying is a stake in the fund manager's ability to perform. If this sounds like a mutual fund, you're right. The ETF structure makes it cheaper than a mutual fund—that is, if it all works out. This raises the question: How would you choose which actively managed ETF is for you if the underlying premise is not an index, but a fund manager's ability to produce a return?

If actively managed funds are based on personality, then who are you going to pick, Warren Buffett? Since he's obviously not in the ETF business, your best bet then for considering an actively managed ETF is a fund offered by a large, well-known investment company with a solid track record. Why would you pick an actively managed ETF from a firm that you don't know much about, especially given the fact that the approach is not totally transparent? There doesn't seem to be a big argument in favor of that.

For top fund companies such as T. Rowe Price, Putnam, or Pimco, actively managed ETFs are all about branding, complementing their existing offerings such as mutual funds. Through brand extension, these fund companies hope to develop a loyal base of investors who will be captured by a one-stop investment shop. If you were going to consider an actively managed ETF, it would make far more sense to look into a fund from a firm with a recognized expertise in an area of the market. For example, as a bond giant in California, Pimco has proven expertise in fixed income. If that investment know-how were applied to an actively managed fund, you might consider it. But even for a firm like Pimco, it's not a slam dunk.

There is a philosophical point with actively managed ETFs that you should grasp before you commit your money. The traditional ETF model has a very rigid structure based on closely following an index. Actively managed ETFs, which are all about the manager's expertise to make good investment choices, have stretched the horizon of what can be called an ETF. If you're a traditional ETF investor, you will probably have a hard time making this leap.

The brand appeal of a large firm, however, will probably capture the attention of some investors who are attracted by past performance figures or intriguing investment hypotheses. However, actively managed ETFs are not like other funds with low fees and high transparency. The differentiation of actively managed funds needs to be explained not only in the fine print, but on the regulatory level so that investors can discern the difference in the strategies of these funds versus other ETF offerings. Otherwise there exists the risk that investors will not fully understand these funds.

Consider the Dent Tactical ETF (DENT) from AdvisorShares, which we have dubbed the dumbest ETF of 2009. Launched in September of that year, DENT is an actively managed ETF with "five key attributes": proprietary demographic analysis, tactical investment approach, risk mitigation process, management expertise, and active management. For all this criteria, you get to pay an expense ratio of 1.56 percent and a management fee of 0.95 percent.

DENT clearly has taken complexity in ETF methodology to a ridiculous level. Moreover, this high-cost ETF adjusts assets at the manager's prerogative, and daily holdings are published only after the close of the trading day. So much for transparency, a fundamental principle of ETFs.

DENT is also the first actively managed ETF to have other ETFs as its components. Laying fund on top of fund has the effect of layering fee on top of fee as well, making low-cost vehicles into a high-cost offering. While the high fees will certainly be a negative for many investors, the fund's strategy is even more troubling. DENT promises to use its five key attributes to track "the overall trend of the U.S. and global economies and how consumer spending patterns may change based on this analysis." In an industry that is proud of transparency, this is as opaque as a brick wall. In our opinion, if it's not clear how a fund is selecting its components, then who knows what you would end up holding a few months later. A much better investment strategy is to buy a variety of ETFs, mutual funds, and other investment vehicles in order to pursue your long-term goals.

You need to ask yourself: How much more could an actively managed ETF return—taking into account its higher fees and costs, and a greater degree of uncertainty—compared to a passively indexed ETF? Would the difference in return make up for the extra risk that you would have to shoulder? If you are going to commit part of your investment funds to an active fund, you need to look at these vehicles with discernment.

In Chapter 1, we discussed the three must-know types of ETFs: domestic, international, and derivative. Theoretically, all three categories could contain both passive and active funds (and ETFs that fall somewhere in between). What's the lesson here? You can't rely on a name alone to tell you what you're getting. You have to understand the objective, whether the approach is passive or active, and the construction of the index, whether U.S. equity, international equity, or derivatives. Personal investment choices will be yours to make. If you are an active-minded, discerning investor, you would probably have less of a need to buy an active ETF. After all, you are taking an active approach. Why would you want to hand over your portfolio to a manager of a fund that lacks transparency?

There are other funds that may make good choices in your port-folio, including some of the custom and dynamic offerings that are based on smart indexing. Although these funds may be marginally more expensive, they could very well be a good deal if the perfor-mance pans out. Many of these funds appear to be good candidates for offering a more balanced way for approaching investment, particu-larly in specific sectors. If your investment horizon is the medium or long term, meaning at least a quarter and up to a few years, then the custom and dynamic ETFs are probably worth your consideration. Keep in mind, though, that if you have a shorter time frame, higher fees associated with some funds can get expensive with more frequent trading.

If we have learned one thing about ETFs over the past decade, it is that there will be a Darwinian effect as offerings proliferate. Only the fittest (i.e., the most liquid) will survive. So what will it be for the fund you've chosen? When it is released into the market, will it gallop across the open plains of investment opportunity? Will it get attacked by competitors? Or will it starve from lack of investor inter-est, and wither and die? The best way to protect yourself and your investment is with education and awareness.

Looking Ahead

As more people become interested in ETFs and continue to take money out of mutual funds (which occurred even in the darkest days of the recession, when investors headed for cover), fund companies are going to look for even more ways to attract investors. To do that, they will keep pumping out proprietary funds, whether active or pas-sive. So what might we see in the future? In order to venture a guess, we look at the notable events of the recent past, including BlackRock's purchase of iShares in a $13.5 billion deal. Clearly, the big players in investment are getting involved in ETFs. With firms such as Schwab and Ameritrade offering an array of services from brokerage to mutual funds and now proprietary ETFs, it seems only a matter of time before Fidelity gets on board—whether it goes it alone or makes an acqui-sition. Therefore, look for more brand name companies to develop

ETFs to keep investors in-house through expanded offerings. It's a logical progression that shows no sign of abating.

As more ETFs are launched and new types of funds are created, there is a veritable feast of choices now spread out before you. Before you take a bite of a more exotic offering, however, you need to understand just what is in a particular fund. If there is a lack of transparency in either the fund construction or how an investment objective is executed, you might decide to pass. After all, there are plenty of other investment possibilities on the table.

Part II

ASSET ALLOCATION
STRATEGIES

Chapter 4

Building a Portfolio Using ETFs

On the temple of Apollo at Delphi were inscribed two pieces of wisdom: "Know thyself" and "Nothing to excess." These two staples of Greek philosophy were meant to advise the many pilgrims who passed through that ancient threshold, but their enduring wisdom can be well applied in today's evolving investment environment.

Regarding the first piece of wisdom, ask yourself: What kind of investor are you?

Are you actively involved, with your eye on the market every day? Or are you more hands-off? You may go through various phases at different points in your life, leaning more toward one investment style over another for any number of reasons, from personal circumstances to market conditions. Whatever phase you are in at the moment, there are ETFs to suit you. In order for those funds to work for you, however, you must analyze their approach and whether their objectives meet your investment needs.

For example, as stated in Chapter 3, if you are actively involved in the market, there is no need for you to choose a fund that is actively managed. Plus, if you are an active investor, you are probably trading frequently. If so, then an actively managed fund that carries a higher fee would not be a good match for you. An actively managed fund, however, may appeal to the hands-off investor who has neither the time nor the inclination to manage his or her own portfolio.

The more active you are as an investor with frequent trades, the more fees will be important to you. (You don't want fees associated with a fund to eat into your returns.) With a hands-off approach, fees may not be as much of an issue; in fact, you may willingly pay a higher fee for a fund with a manager who is executing an investment approach that appeals to you. Also keep in mind that narrowly focused and specialized ETFs (e.g., international health care) will typically charge a higher fee than a passively indexed, broad-based fund.

Liquidity of a fund, while always a consideration, is especially important for the active investor. When you want to get out of a position, you don't want a lack of trading volume to become an issue. The hands-off investor with a long-term perspective is less concerned about liquidity as long as there is adequate volume in the fund.

As we discussed in Part I, the ETF mold is evolving with a host of products available. The temptation may be for you to jump in with a fund that has an appealing objective or a good track record without considering whether that ETF is the best match for you and your particular investment approach.

In this discussion, we are going to look at three basic types of investors: the Super Hands-On Active Trader, the High-Touch Satellite Investor, and the Portfolio Builder, which also includes three subcategories of Core Holder, Armchair Investor, and Autopilot Investor. Chances are you will find yourself somewhere in this investor lineup.

The Super Hands-On Active Trader

At the far end of the spectrum is the Super Hands-On Active Trader, a professional who uses ETFs to hedge a position or to gain exposure intraday. The key phrase here is *intraday*. The Super Hands-On Active Trader is moving into and out of funds within a single trading day as part of an overall market strategy, particularly to hedge a position.

Highly active and involved in the market, the Super Hands-On Active Trader may use leveraged funds that seek to deliver double or triple the performance of a particular index. For example, if the trader wants to take a long position in the financial sector intraday, one choice might be Direxion's Financial Bull 3X Shares (FAS), which seeks to return the daily investment results, before fees and expenses, of 300 percent of the price performance of the Russell 1000 Financial Services Index. If the trader wants intraday short exposure, the trader might consider Direxion's Financial Bear 3X Shares (FAZ), which seeks daily investment results, before fees and expenses, of 300 percent of the inverse (opposite) of the price performance of the Russell 1000 Financial Services Index.

We've said this before, but it bears repeating: Leverage funds such as the FAX and FAZ are only for daily trading—not for investing. (As Direxion states on its web site, "These funds are intended for use only by sophisticated investors who: (a) understand the risks associated with the use of leverage; (b) understand the consequences of seeking daily leveraged investment results; and (c) intend to actively monitor and manage their investments." http://www.direxionshares.com/education .html.) Further emphasizing their use intraday, shares of leveraged funds are turned over more than once a day.

For the Super Hands-On Active Trader, leveraged funds are important tools to use as part of an overall trading strategy. Precision is of the utmost importance. A fund must perform as expected and track exactly what it is supposed to track. Because frequent positions are taken intraday, moving in and out of funds in a matter of hours, liquidity is very important. (See Figure 4.1.)

The High-Touch Satellite Investor

The next type of investor definitely takes an active approach, but not to the degree of the Super Hands-On Active Trader. The High-Touch Satellite Investor uses ETFs to augment an existing portfolio

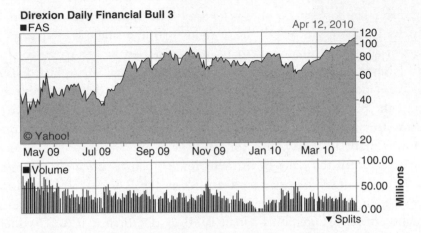

Figure 4.1 Direxion's Financial Bull 3X shares (FAS) shows strong volume in the tens of millions of shares, providing ample liquidity for traders intraday.
SOURCE: Reproduced with permission of Yahoo! Inc. © 2010 Yahoo! Inc. YAHOO! and the YAHOO! logo are registered trademarks of Yahoo! Inc.

that may be complete unto itself. For this investor, the addition of ETFs gives the investor hands-on access to daily market fluctuations. For the High-Touch Satellite Investor, it's all about executing a strategy, rather than relying on someone else to manage the portfolio.

ETFs allow the High-Touch Satellite Investor to make short-term directional trades, with "satellite" positions that are separate from his or her main portfolio. The High-Touch Satellite Investor has a core portfolio that is spread across a variety of assets: stocks, investment bonds, mutual funds, and real estate. Rather than buying or selling portfolio holdings, the High-Touch Satellite Investor sees ETFs as a way to make "sector bets" based on opinions regarding the likelihood of one sector or another to outperform the overall market. The investor buys ETFs because of the appeal of gaining market exposure through a vehicle that trades daily on an exchange, enabling him or her to target a specific portion of the market.

What's important to note here is that the High-Touch Satellite Investor is not using ETFs as core holdings—or the "meat and potatoes," if you will—of the portfolio. Rather, these satellite holdings provide exposure that is hard to gain using mutual funds. For the

High-Touch Satellite Investor, ETFs that offer exposure to particular sectors—such as telecommunications, health care, or consumer staples—are appealing for their ease of entry, relatively low fees, and liquidity. This investor will favor funds that have low fees and high liquidity, such as the iShares Dow Jones US Financial Sector ETF (IYF), or the popular bullion-backed SPDR Gold Shares ETF (GLD). Both of these ETFs offer unique exposure to different areas of the marketplace that an active investor may want to monitor on a daily basis.

What might a High-Touch Satellite Investor look like? Consider the young professional who has a long-term portfolio that over the course of his or her investment life will hopefully grow and eventually provide income starting at age 65. In the short term, however, this investor has some ideas regarding investment opportunities to pursue. Instead of tampering with a long-term portfolio or trying to engage in stock-picking, the High-Touch Satellite Investor uses ETFs to gain exposure to a sector.

The Portfolio Builder

This next type of investor seeks to build a complete portfolio using ETFs. It may be that this investor has a nest egg to invest or has a portfolio to rebuild after being all or mostly in cash during a market downturn, such as we experienced during the 2007–2008 financial crisis. For the Portfolio Builder, the ETF *is* the investment philosophy. In other words, the Portfolio Builder has made a strategic decision to build a portfolio largely using ETFs for both long-term core positions and short-term strategic holdings. As we will discuss, the Portfolio Builder includes three subcategories of investors who use ETFs to construct their portfolio, but with an increasingly hands-off approach.

In general, all Portfolio Builders have core positions that may be amassed using broad-based funds such as the SPDR S&P 500 ETF (SPY), PowerShares QQQ Trust (QQQQ), or the Diamonds Trust Series 1 ETF (DIA), which tracks the Dow Jones Industrial Average. These passive indexed funds provide access to market direction for the long term with high transparency in a predictable fashion. The Portfolio Builder may also choose ETFs that provide access to investment styles such as large-cap value or mid-cap growth much like a mutual fund—but with greater transparency, lower fees, and intraday trading. Examples would include the iShares S&P 500 Value Index ETF (IVE) or Vanguard Mid-Cap Growth ETF (VOT). As Figure 4.2 shows, (VOT) presents itself in much the same way as a mutual fund, using the familiar 9-box grid or "style box" to show how a domestic stock fund's holdings are distributed by primary investment style (growth, value, or blend) and market capitalization category (large-, mid-, and small-cap companies).

Using ETFs as the core of the portfolio allows the Portfolio Builder to "stay on the highway," as we like to say, following overall market direction. In addition, the Portfolio Builder uses ETFs to gain exposure to particular sectors or to explore investment opportunities through commodity or currency ETFs. Long-term or short-term, the Portfolio Builder is constructing an entire portfolio using ETFs. The Portfolio Builder typically is trading less frequently than more active investors; therefore, fees and liquidity are not as crucial as with the more active investors and traders.

More of a concern for the Portfolio Builder is the unintended effect of overlap, creating pockets of concentration in one particular

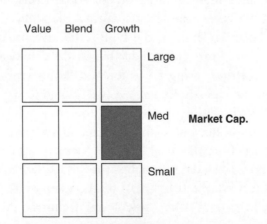
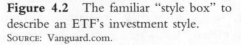

Figure 4.2   The familiar "style box" to describe an ETF's investment style.
Source: Vanguard.com.

Table 4.1   Top holdings in the PowerShares Dynamic Technology Sector (PTF)

Western Digital Corp.	2.62%	Cognizant Technology Solutions Corp.	2.52%
Tyco Electronics Ltd.	2.60%	CA Inc.	2.48%
Xilinx Inc.	2.57%	Apple Inc.	2.47%
EMC Corp.	2.53%	Microsoft Corp.	2.43%
Red Hat Inc.	2.53%	International Business Machines Corp.	2.41%

Note: As of 1/26/2010
SOURCE: InvescoPowerShares.com.

stock. For example, let's say the Portfolio Builder has a core holding in QQQQ. In late January 2010, the top holding in QQQQ was Apple Inc., accounting for 15.6 percent of the portfolio. If this investor then bought the PowerShares Dynamic Technology Sector Portfolio (PTF), it would be important to know that Apple is among its top holdings (as shown in Table 4.1), accounting for roughly 2.5 percent in January 2010. This may or may not be more Apple exposure than the Portfolio Builder wants to have. The point is the investor must be aware of top holdings in all ETFs and how that impacts his or her portfolio.

The Core Holder

The Core Holder is the first subcategory of Portfolio Builder that we will discuss. The Core Holder typically owns 12 to 16 ETFs, with broad-based funds such as the SPY, DIA, or the QQQQ as core holdings. Although this investor is hands-off—trading very infrequently—he or she needs to understand what these core holdings represent; for example, that the DIA will track the Dow components and the QQQQ is very heavily weighted toward technology.

The Core Holder then uses a few ETFs to layer on additional exposure to certain sectors or subsectors. For example, in addition to the technology exposure of the QQQQ, a Core Holder may decide to buy a subsector fund that enables this investor to gain exposure to semiconductors or the Internet. As with any Portfolio Builder, the issue will be overlap. However, by using targeted subsector funds, the Core Holder can minimize overlap by seeking exposure just to those types of companies that he or she wants to hold.

The Core Holder will most likely follow a basic indexing strategy such as market capitalization or perhaps a customized approach that weights on the basis of revenue or dividends. High transparency appeals to the Core Holder, provided that he or she does the necessary research to understand a fund's objective and to examine its core holdings. (Keep in mind the "Basic Tenets of ETF Investing," as discussed in Chapter 1: Appropriateness, Liquidity, and Concentration.)

The Core Holder, like other investors, would do well to consider all alternatives within an investment theme or sector. As more ETFs are launched, fees are being driven down as lower-cost alternatives are introduced. Although "first-mover status" is important from a marketing standpoint, there may be a cheaper alternative to consider. For example, the iShares MSCI Emerging Markets Index Fund (EEM) was introduced in April 2003 and has an expense ratio of 0.72 percent. The Vanguard Emerging Markets ETF (VWO), introduced in March 2005, has an expense ratio of only 0.27 percent. Although the funds are not exactly alike, investors would do well to consider which fund offers the exposure they desire along with an affordable fee.

The Armchair Investor

A second subcategory within Portfolio Builder is the Armchair Investor. Like the Core Holder, the Armchair Investor holds broad-based ETFs to gain exposure to the major indexes. However, the Armchair Investor is less involved on a regular basis than the Core Holder.

The Armchair Investor is aware of sector exposure; for example, using QQQQ to invest in technology, but that is about as granular as it gets. The Armchair Investor is not looking to slice-and-dice a sector down to subsector components in order to gain short-term exposure, unlike the Core Holder.

Typically, the Armchair Investor would have about eight ETFs that he or she looks at quarterly, since that is when most ETFs are rebalanced. At each quarter, the Armchair Investor looks at performance and decides whether or not to make a change. Although trading is very infrequent, the Armchair Investor likes the flexibility that ETFs offer in case of lifestyle changes or dramatic market shifts.

The Autopilot Investor

This last type of Portfolio Builder investor is the least active in his or her own portfolio management. Autopilot Investors use ETFs but are most likely to do so as part of a buy-and-hold approach. They typically use funds that track the broad-based indexes as well as those that have a particular investment style such as large-cap growth or international.

Because the Autopilot Investor is so hands-off, he or she may be interested in pursuing funds that promise to generate alpha—or performance over and above the underlying index benchmark. Therefore, the Autopilot Investor would be a good candidate for dynamic or actively managed ETFs, which we discussed in Chapter 3. For Autopilot Investors, having a fund manager do all the work—albeit in return for a higher fee—is preferable than trying to do the portfolio management themselves. The Autopilot Investor's mantra is "I am much more comfortable putting my faith in a smart strategy than trying to understand it myself."

Investment Continuum

As an investor, you may slide in and out of these phases. You may be more active at one point in your life and more hands-off and passive at another. Therefore, your self-knowledge, as stated at the opening of the chapter, is key to understanding where you are along the investment continuum. You may also be able to switch phases—for example, becoming more active by choosing sectors and subsectors—without tampering with your core holdings.

Whatever your investment approach is, broad-based ETFs such as the SPY, QQQQ, or DIA can be important building blocks for your portfolio. Although these ETFs, as described in Chapter 3, are considered to be the plain vanilla within an increasing array of fund choices, passively indexed funds are easy and low-cost ways to gain broad market exposure. These are the funds that can "keep you on the highway" and tracking the overall market. The last thing you want to do is put together a portfolio consisting only of narrowly defined exotic choices that crash while the overall market is rallying. By using the plain-vanilla indexes at the core of your portfolio, you can pursue other funds that have the potential to increase your overall performance.

Consider the QQQQ, which is one of the most highly monitored and frequently traded ETFs. Composed of the largest domestic and international nonfinancial companies listed on NASDAQ, the QQQQ as we've said before is tech-heavy, with nearly two-thirds allocated in tech stocks. Other sectors represented in the QQQQ are consumer discretionary (at 14.28 percent as of late January 2010) and health care (16.36 percent). Smaller allocations are made to industrials, telecommunication services, consumer staples, and materials.

QQQQ has a high correlation to other major benchmark indexes such as the S&P 500 and the Dow Jones Industrial Average, providing long-term shareholders with a way to follow market trends. In addition, the QQQQ can also be used by short-term investors to hedge market movements. Although there is a high degree of correlation between the QQQQ and the S&P 500, the composition of the two indexes (and hence the funds that track them) is very different.

The QQQQ, like other large passively indexed ETFs, has an attractive level of liquidity, keeping price spread narrow and allowing for ease of trading. For many reasons ETFs that track the broad market, such as the SPY, QQQQ, and the DIA (see Figure 4.3) are good building blocks for investor portfolios.

The Importance of Diversification: Nothing to Excess

Now we turn to the second piece of wisdom on the temple of Apollo at Delphi: "Nothing to excess." With this insight in mind, we begin our discussion regarding diversification. Although this concept has been around for a while, the wisdom of this approach is timeless.

The basic premise of diversification is that it's a good idea to hold a variety of investments in your portfolio so that losses in one particular holding do not derail your investment plan. If you are like many investors, your familiarity with diversification may end there. What you may not realize is the way your investments are diversified between and within various types of assets is likely to have a greater

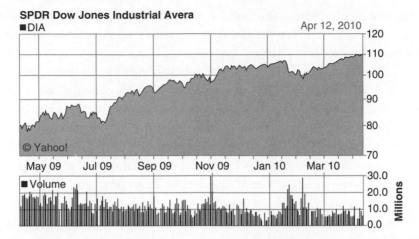

Figure 4.3 The strong volume in the DIA makes it—like the SPY and QQQQ—a popular choice for a core portfolio holding.
Source: Reproduced with permission of Yahoo! Inc. © 2010 Yahoo! Inc. YAHOO! and the YAHOO! logo are registered trademarks of Yahoo! Inc.

impact on your investment returns than virtually any other factor. There is more to building a diversified portfolio than pulling together a collection of mutual funds or ETFs. You must also consider the portfolio's balance of asset classes, the types of individual securities represented, the likelihood that the holdings will perform in different patterns than one another, and how they correlate to your total holdings.

The first consideration is diversification by asset class. Nearly all financial assets fall into one of five categories: stocks, bonds, commodities, real estate, or cash. These five classes have very different risk/reward profiles: Stocks offer the greatest potential payoff and volatility; bonds offer lower return potential with modest volatility; commodities typically offer less reward than stocks, but less inflation risk than bonds; real estate risk and reward are tied to the amount of leverage you use; and cash offers near-total stability and negligible potential return. Bonds offer the greatest current income, usually followed by real estate, cash, and then stocks.

Finally, different environments are likely to affect the returns of each asset class in different ways. For example, a weakening economy generally leads to problems in the stock market, while economic weakness usually boosts the bond market. Because each of the classes tends to behave differently, holding a portion of your assets in each can help smooth out your overall returns.

Other factors might also affect your asset allocation decision, including your risk tolerance. If worries about market volatility keep you up at night, you may be better off shifting some of your assets from stocks to bonds or cash. Before you take that step, however, make sure you understand the trade-offs involved, including that your investments might lose ground to inflation. Likewise, the amount of assets you have to invest could affect your decision about how much to invest in stocks, bonds, commodities, real estate, and cash. In general, if you have more assets, you can afford to hold fewer assets in stocks, since your need for growth is less. Conversely, if you have smaller savings you may need to take on greater risk of market volatility in order to increase your chance of generating enough growth to last through retirement. (Remember that assuming greater volatility risk also increases the possibility of losses.)

You can also maximize your portfolio's risk-adjusted return by diversifying among different types of investments within each asset class. It's relatively simple to judge how likely it is that a fund will move independently of the broad market: Look for a fund's "R-squared" ratio (which is available on web sites such as Morningstar or Yahoo! Finance). This number, which will be between 0 and 100, tells you the percentage of the fund's movement that is explained by movements in a given index, usually the S&P 500. If a fund has an R-squared of 100, its returns have moved in the same direction as the index, without exception, during the time period being examined (which is usually the trailing three years). As you might expect, the SPY has an R-squared of 100, since it tracks the S&P 500. An R-squared of 0 indicates that no portion of the fund's fluctuation is attributed to the index (see Table 4.2).

One way to diversify within a stock portfolio is to invest the core portion—say, 50 to 75 percent of equity assets—in funds that are likely to produce relatively high correlation with the stock market as a whole, and then to invest the remainder in a selection of different funds with a good chance of moving in the other direction when the broad market retreats. Such funds might include those that invest in

Table 4.2 Risk statistics for SPY (top) show an R-squared rating of 100. By comparison, Vanguard Small Cap Value ETF (VBR) (bottom) has an R-squared rating of 87.21

Statistic	SPY	Category
R-squared (against Standard Index)	100.00	95.76

Statistic	VBR	Category
R-squared (against Standard Index)	87.21	81.07

SOURCE: Yahoo! Finance.

mid- and small-cap stocks. A properly diversified portfolio should hold some exposure to small and medium-sized stocks as well as market heavyweights.

Small-cap stocks historically have generated higher average returns than large-cap stocks, but they also have been more likely to post severe short-term losses. Because small caps do not move in lockstep with large caps, holding a combination of both can make an overall portfolio less volatile than a portfolio with only stocks of one size or the other.

Diversification also can be obtained through funds that invest in international stocks. Stocks that trade in a foreign country are affected by different factors than U.S. stocks, so they tend to move in different patterns than domestic shares. Another diversification move is to invest in sectors or types of securities with low correlation to the overall U.S. market. Stocks in certain economic sectors and industries tend to follow different cycles than the overall market. They include real estate, natural resources, energy, defense, precious metals, utilities, and health care, among others. Funds that invest in different types of equity securities, such as convertibles, preferred stock, or distressed securities, also can provide diversification benefits.

Just as with stocks, investing in various types of bonds can help you to pursue more return from the asset class without substantially increasing your risk of losses. A diversified bond portfolio might hold three-quarters or so of the portfolio's bond assets in a core mix of intermediate-term Treasury bonds and high-quality corporate and government agency bonds, which is then supplemented with smaller allocations to other sectors in the bond market. For example, most fixed-income investors, including retirees, should consider a modest stake in high-yield bonds. Bonds issued by companies with relatively weak finances can provide higher current income than government or high-quality corporate bonds, as well as the potential for capital appreciation. However, they also bring a greater risk of losses than most other bonds. That said, high-yield bonds do provide a degree of protection against rising interest rates, which typically weaken returns for other types of bonds.

Finally, some investors may want to add a touch of exposure to international bonds. Like foreign stocks, foreign bonds tend to move in different cycles than their domestic counterparts, potentially boosting returns when the U.S. bond market slumps. Foreign bonds also may offer higher yields than domestic bonds. However, foreign bonds can carry much greater risk of losses than U.S. bonds, so retired investors in particular should keep exposure to overseas fixed income investments to a minimum.

Intelligent Diversification with ETFs

Most do-it-yourself investors know that diversification is one of the keys to better portfolio performance, and ETFs are an easy way to add exposure to a wide range of stock and bond indexes, industry sectors, and developed and emerging markets overseas. In addition, there are dozens of innovative ETFs that provide access to investment strategies and areas of the market—such as currencies and commodities—that used to be either largely off-limits or extremely difficult for do-it-yourself investors.

All investments carry a certain amount of risk. From low-risk Treasury bonds to highly speculative initial public offerings, there is always a chance that an initial investment will decline in value. The bad news for investors is that there is one type of risk—known as "systematic" or "market" risk—that cannot really be controlled. Interest rates, wars, weather, and political instability fit into this category. The good news, however, is that the other type of risk—sometimes referred to as "unsystematic" risk—can be minimized using diversification.

Let's take a look at an example of why diversification is such a powerful tool. Imagine that your portfolio consists of a single fund: a biotechnology sector fund such as the iShares Nasdaq Biotechnology Fund (IBB). If the biotech industry booms, the value of your single-fund portfolio will soar along with it. However, with this one fund you are also vulnerable to the cycles of this volatile growth industry. Therefore, if you invested half your assets in a broad-market stock fund, such as the SPDR S&P 500 ETF (SPY), then only part of your portfolio would have been subject to the boom and bust cycles of the biotech sector. Adding a bond ETF would decrease your risk even further, because stocks and bonds respond differently as economic and market conditions change.

Over-diversification, however, can offset the benefits of a well-constructed, well-diversified portfolio. When assets are spread across too many investments, the potential for a big gain to boost overall performance is diminished. In addition, a big portfolio can be difficult to manage and can generate excessive trading fees as investors tweak their positions.

In summary, as you build and manage your portfolio, begin by looking first at yourself. Identify the type of investor you are based upon your goals, as well as your time and inclination to devote to the market. No matter how active or passive you are, whether you have a core portfolio composed of several types of assets or your holdings are all ETFs, there are funds for you. In short, know thyself. As your portfolio grows and changes over time, keep aware of the balance among the assets with "nothing to excess" so that you remain well diversified to increase your chances of success and mitigate the impact of a downturn in one particular area.

Chapter 5

Trading: Navigating the Storm

L ooking over the shoulder of a lead market maker, the opening bell is the eye of the hurricane. Preceded by a flurry of pricing and orders, there is a moment of quiet when the unbridled forces of demand hit supply. In that brief space where anything goes, this collision can lift, twist, and separate a fund's price from the foundations that hold it. As each component springs to life, a hundred hands lift from within an ETF's basket—grabbing, catching, and securing a wavering market price. If all goes well, the fund is anchored. The market maker looks around, surveys the damage, and determines where she must buy or sell to make things whole. After hedging her bets and making one last check for market conditions, she steps into the fury of regular trading.

For the outsider, the trading environment can be as unfamiliar as it is overwhelming. Amidst the chaos, however, there is both practice and protocol. In this chapter, we are going to defuse some of the mystery and help you to understand the dynamics at work in the market so you can learn when and why you can find the most opportune times to place your trades.

In order to truly understand the impact of the market open on an ETF, we need to take a step back. It begins with the listing process as an ETF is "born." In the simplest terms, it starts with an ETF issuer with an idea for a product, whether based on a well-known benchmark such as the S&P 500 or an index of its own. In order to bring that ETF to life, the product must be presented to the people who are eligible to act as the lead market makers on the New York Stock Exchange (NYSE) or NASDAQ. For the most part, ETFs are seeded by the firms that are going to act as the lead market makers, the ones who will bring the funds to life. The lead market maker will create the ETF in the literal and figurative sense, from nothing more than an idea to a tradable product.

The lead market makers are among a small group of firms that are eligible to act in this capacity, which involves the obligation to make a two-sided market and the privilege of creating and redeeming shares of the fund. The lead market maker acts as both a market participant and as a principal; in other words, trading on behalf of the firm's account and providing liquidity for customers. The most important function of the lead market maker, however, is continuously offering a two-sided market throughout the trading day. As part of that responsibility, the lead market maker sets the pricing of the fund at the opening.

Long before the market opens, the National Securities Clearing Corporation (NSCC) delivers a listing of all ETFs and all of their contents—securities, shares, and cash. When the lead market maker arrives each morning, he utilizes that list along with a live data feed with bid/ask price quotes in the premarket to calculate the value of everything that's in a particular fund. His calculations determine the net asset value (NAV) of the ETF before trading begins. The process is beautiful in its simplicity and transparency: The contents of the fund and the bid/ask prices of the components produce the NAV.

Let's say that the NAV of a particular fund is around $27. In the premarket, the bid/ask prices of each fund component fluctuate, which also impacts the NAV—now quoted at $27.10, then $26.95, back to $27.00, and so forth. In the meantime, opening orders to buy or sell the ETF are being entered right up to the last second. Some are orders to buy or sell at the market; others specify a particular price.

This is the price-discovery phase, which occurs on two levels. One is the price discovery that happens within the components of the fund; for example, each individual stock in a domestic equity ETF. This activity in the underlying components will move the NAV in the premarket, up and down, until the opening bell. On top of that there is price discovery for the ETF itself, as orders are entered. As all these things occur at once, the market maker is establishing the bid/ask spread for the ETF, which is also influenced by the market maker's own inventory of shares to buy or sell. The bid/ask spread has to be sufficiently wide in the premarket to allow the NAV to fluctuate. Setting these prices is the biggest job requirement of the lead market makers.

The flurry of activity reaches a peak just before the market opens. The eye of the hurricane is approaching. The bid/ask spread that was relatively wide begins to narrow as opening orders are processed. The more liquid a fund is, the closer its price gets to the NAV. For some highly liquid funds like the SPDR S&P 500 ETF (SPY), it happens instantaneously. For less liquid products, the process of digesting opening orders and establishing trading in the underlying components takes longer; therefore, the spread between the price of the ETF and its NAV will remain wide for an extended period of time.

The point here for you to understand is that the market open is a period of price discovery. In order for this process to occur, market makers must keep the bid/ask spread sufficiently wide. As a result, there is inherently more volatility in pricing. The key to this process is liquidity. If there is sufficient liquidity for the ETF and its underlying components, then price discovery is going to be efficient. If there is little or no liquidity, it will not work. During the price-discovery period, the ETF may not trade in line with its NAV. For these reasons, you don't want to trade near the open market. In fact, the rule of thumb is not to be involved in buying or selling ETFs in the first half hour of the market.

Timing is everything. After the market has had time to digest the opening, you should have a good window for trading between 10:00 and 11:30 A.M. Eastern Time. The lunch hour is not ideal because

activity can taper off. Why trade when the market i...
not have to? Another opportunity is between 2:3...
Eastern Time. Just make sure that you avoid the last...
when pricing can be affected again as the lead mark...
their portfolios.

Remember, your objective is to maximize the inh...
of ETFs as low-cost, transparent investment vehicles...
not only want to pick funds that closely track their...
you also want to be active in the market when ETF...
to have a tight spread between the price of the fun...
During the trading day, the spread will be kept in lin...
trage. Professional traders engage in arbitrage to try...
price discrepancies between ETFs and their underlyi...
As they buy one and sell the other, this activity...
narrow the gaps between fund prices and NAVs. Fu...
trage trading helps to increase liquidity in an ETF, w...
as you execute your more straightforward trades,...
selling ETF shares.

Lead market makers are not the only ones invo...
market. Authorized market participants also are allow...
redeem shares. This not only adds to the liquidity of...
helps to keep bid/ask spreads in line with the fund's...
it this way: What would the motivation be for mark...
were the only ones involved in share creation a...
Obviously, they would be motivated by their own...
make as much money as possible, and therefore wou...
spreads as wide as possible. You can observe this in th...
for which there is little or no competition for order...
maker can keep spreads wide and not worry about...
somewhere for share creation and redemption. With...
the market maker may be the only game in town.

With a liquid ETF that trades millions or even...
of shares a day, competition changes the pricing dyn...
the market maker selling at, say, a two-cent premiu...
market participant comes in who is willing to sell sh...
Whoever has the best pricing will attract the order...
penny a share on 5,000 shares won't pay the rent. Bu...

Chapter 5

Trading: Navigating the Storm

L ooking over the shoulder of a lead market maker, the opening bell is the eye of the hurricane. Preceded by a flurry of pricing and orders, there is a moment of quiet when the unbridled forces of demand hit supply. In that brief space where anything goes, this collision can lift, twist, and separate a fund's price from the foundations that hold it. As each component springs to life, a hundred hands lift from within an ETF's basket—grabbing, catching, and securing a wavering market price. If all goes well, the fund is anchored. The market maker looks around, surveys the damage, and determines where she must buy or sell to make things whole. After hedging her bets and making one last check for market conditions, she steps into the fury of regular trading.

For the outsider, the trading environment can be as unfamiliar as it is overwhelming. Amidst the chaos, however, there is both practice and protocol. In this chapter, we are going to defuse some of the mystery and help you to understand the dynamics at work in the market so you can learn when and why you can find the most opportune times to place your trades.

In order to truly understand the impact of the market open on an ETF, we need to take a step back. It begins with the listing process as an ETF is "born." In the simplest terms, it starts with an ETF issuer with an idea for a product, whether based on a well-known benchmark such as the S&P 500 or an index of its own. In order to bring that ETF to life, the product must be presented to the people who are eligible to act as the lead market makers on the New York Stock Exchange (NYSE) or NASDAQ. For the most part, ETFs are seeded by the firms that are going to act as the lead market makers, the ones who will bring the funds to life. The lead market maker will create the ETF in the literal and figurative sense, from nothing more than an idea to a tradable product.

The lead market makers are among a small group of firms that are eligible to act in this capacity, which involves the obligation to make a two-sided market and the privilege of creating and redeeming shares of the fund. The lead market maker acts as both a market participant and as a principal; in other words, trading on behalf of the firm's account and providing liquidity for customers. The most important function of the lead market maker, however, is continuously offering a two-sided market throughout the trading day. As part of that responsibility, the lead market maker sets the pricing of the fund at the opening.

Long before the market opens, the National Securities Clearing Corporation (NSCC) delivers a listing of all ETFs and all of their contents—securities, shares, and cash. When the lead market maker arrives each morning, he utilizes that list along with a live data feed with bid/ask price quotes in the premarket to calculate the value of everything that's in a particular fund. His calculations determine the net asset value (NAV) of the ETF before trading begins. The process is beautiful in its simplicity and transparency: The contents of the fund and the bid/ask prices of the components produce the NAV.

Let's say that the NAV of a particular fund is around $27. In the premarket, the bid/ask prices of each fund component fluctuate, which also impacts the NAV—now quoted at $27.10, then $26.95, back to $27.00, and so forth. In the meantime, opening orders to buy or sell the ETF are being entered right up to the last second. Some are orders to buy or sell at the market; others specify a particular price.

This is the price-discovery phase, which occurs on two levels. One is the price discovery that happens within the components of the fund; for example, each individual stock in a domestic equity ETF. This activity in the underlying components will move the NAV in the premarket, up and down, until the opening bell. On top of that there is price discovery for the ETF itself, as orders are entered. As all these things occur at once, the market maker is establishing the bid/ask spread for the ETF, which is also influenced by the market maker's own inventory of shares to buy or sell. The bid/ask spread has to be sufficiently wide in the premarket to allow the NAV to fluctuate. Setting these prices is the biggest job requirement of the lead market makers.

The flurry of activity reaches a peak just before the market opens. The eye of the hurricane is approaching. The bid/ask spread that was relatively wide begins to narrow as opening orders are processed. The more liquid a fund is, the closer its price gets to the NAV. For some highly liquid funds like the SPDR S&P 500 ETF (SPY), it happens instantaneously. For less liquid products, the process of digesting opening orders and establishing trading in the underlying components takes longer; therefore, the spread between the price of the ETF and its NAV will remain wide for an extended period of time.

The point here for you to understand is that the market open is a period of price discovery. In order for this process to occur, market makers must keep the bid/ask spread sufficiently wide. As a result, there is inherently more volatility in pricing. The key to this process is liquidity. If there is sufficient liquidity for the ETF and its underlying components, then price discovery is going to be efficient. If there is little or no liquidity, it will not work. During the price-discovery period, the ETF may not trade in line with its NAV. For these reasons, you don't want to trade near the open market. In fact, the rule of thumb is not to be involved in buying or selling ETFs in the first half hour of the market.

Timing is everything. After the market has had time to digest the opening, you should have a good window for trading between 10:00 and 11:30 A.M. Eastern Time. The lunch hour is not ideal because activity can taper off. Why trade when the market is thin if you do not have to? Another opportunity is between 2:30 and 3:30 P.M. Eastern Time. Just make sure that you avoid the last half hour or so when pricing can be affected again as the lead market makers adjust their portfolios.

Remember, your objective is to maximize the inherent advantages of ETFs as low-cost, transparent investment vehicles. Therefore, you not only want to pick funds that closely track their underlying value, you also want to be active in the market when ETFs are most likely to have a tight spread between the price of the fund and the NAV. During the trading day, the spread will be kept in line partly by arbitrage. Professional traders engage in arbitrage to try to profit from price discrepancies between ETFs and their underlying components. As they buy one and sell the other, this activity actually helps to narrow the gaps between fund prices and NAVs. Furthermore, arbitrage trading helps to increase liquidity in an ETF, which is beneficial as you execute your more straightforward trades, either buying or selling ETF shares.

Lead market makers are not the only ones involved in the ETF market. Authorized market participants also are allowed to create and redeem shares. This not only adds to the liquidity of the ETF, it also helps to keep bid/ask spreads in line with the fund's value. Think of it this way: What would the motivation be for market makers if they were the only ones involved in share creation and redemption? Obviously, they would be motivated by their own best interest to make as much money as possible, and therefore would keep bid/ask spreads as wide as possible. You can observe this in thinly traded ETFs for which there is little or no competition for order flow. The market maker can keep spreads wide and not worry about order flow going somewhere for share creation and redemption. With an illiquid ETF, the market maker may be the only game in town.

With a liquid ETF that trades millions or even tens of millions of shares a day, competition changes the pricing dynamic. Instead of the market maker selling at, say, a two-cent premium, an authorized market participant comes in who is willing to sell shares for half that. Whoever has the best pricing will attract the order flow. Making a penny a share on 5,000 shares won't pay the rent. But a penny a share on 50 million shares is a lucrative business. In order to capture order volume, spreads are kept as tight as possible. Market makers and authorized market participants do not even care if the fund price is going up or down, as long as there is volume. (It's like the toll booth operator who has no vested interest in whether the traffic moves north or south, as long as the vehicles pay their tolls.) Volume is in everyone's best interest: the market maker who wants to capture as much order flow as possible by offering tight spreads; the investor who wants good liquidity and tight spreads for a fair trade; and the ETF issuer who wants a fund to attract as much investor interest as possible.

Placing Your Trades

When you buy and sell ETFs, consider using limit orders. If you are trying to get into an ETF at a specific price, you can place a limit order to buy at a specific price; for example, where you have determined that there is established support and other buyers are likely to come into the market. Be careful about trying to "bottom fish" by setting a price that's too far below the current market. The market may not retrace enough to hit your limit order to get you in at a specific price. If that happens, the fund could take off without you.

Limit orders can also be used to get out at a specific price; for example, at a resistance level that is above where the market is currently trading. You can also put in a limit order as a protective "stop." If the price of an ETF were to fall enough to hit your sell order, you would be out of the market with a predetermined loss—instead of facing a potential free fall that could compound your losses.

Also keep in mind that buying an ETF is generally a lot less risky than selling because of the incentive system between the issuer and the party that seeds the fund. Rather than delve deeply into this relationship here, what you need to know is that newer funds, for obvious reasons, want their assets to grow. As the ETF grows, the number of shares increases. The problem arises when fund shares are redeemed—and yes, you can redeem back to zero. Therefore, there is an incentive to go positive, not negative, in ETFs, which is going to favor the buyer and attempt to discourage the seller.

Not every day will be an optimal trading day because of the overall market conditions. For example, if the market is very volatile, with big swings in both directions, you should avoid trading. Trading in a market with high volatility is like sailing in extremely choppy seas. It won't make for much of a ride, you could get knocked off course, and you might even get sick. Unless you absolutely have to make the voyage, why risk it? It would be better to wait for calmer seas and clearer direction. When the market is particularly volatile, the spread between the price of an ETF and its NAV can widen, making it less favorable for you to trade. Volatility can also widen the bid/ask spread, which will affect the prices at which you can buy or sell a fund. If volatility is extreme, wild price swings can significantly impact the profitability of your trades.

Avoid days when trading volume is reduced. This is frequently seen around major holidays when participation tends to be less, or when the market is only open a half day. When liquidity is reduced, prices can be affected.

Be Aware of the International Disconnect

We've all seen the image on television: The Space Shuttle launches, propelled higher and higher into the atmosphere by powerful booster rockets. Then the Shuttle disengages, and the rockets are discarded. The Shuttle is on its own, making its way into orbit. Something similar happens with international equity ETFs that are listed on U.S. exchanges while their components trade in overseas markets. When both marketplaces are open, everything is moving in tandem. Then the foreign markets close, and the value of the ETF disconnects from the underlying components. The ETF is on its own.

The ETF may still be moving in the same direction as it was before, but now it's being acted on by the gravitational forces of the marketplace. In other words, what is happening in an international equity ETF after the overseas markets close has far less to do with its underlying components than it does with whatever is impacting the overall market. If at all possible, enter your buy or sell orders for ETFs that hold international or emerging-market stocks when the overseas

Table 5.1 Standard Trading Hours (Excluding Pre/Post Hours)

Exchange	Market Hours
NASDAQ Stock Market Trading Sessions	9:30 A.M. to 4:00 P.M. Eastern Time
NYSE ARCA Equities	9:30 A.M. to 4:00 P.M. Eastern Time
London Stock Exchange	8:00 A.M. to 4:30 P.M. GMT equivalent to 3:00 A.M. to 11:30 A.M. Eastern Time
Euronext	9:00 to 17:30 (5:30 P.M.) CET equivalent to 3:00 A.M. to 11:30 A.M. Eastern Time
Tokyo Stock Exchange	9:00 to 11:00 12:30 to 15:00 (3:00 P.M.) TSE equivalent to 7:00 P.M. to 9:00 P.M. Eastern Time prior day 10:30 P.M. to 1:00 A.M. Eastern Time

exchanges are also open. The London Stock Exchange, for example, closes at 11:30 A.M. Eastern Time (see Table 5.1). However, Asian markets are not open while U.S. stocks are trading. As an investor, you need to be aware of the potential impact of trading hours on your ETFs.

All about Liquidity

Whether you are getting into or out of the market, you need ample liquidity to execute your trade. The last thing you want is a price dislocation caused by a lack of liquidity. As we discussed in Chapter 1, a number of factors determine liquidity. To recap, there is primary liquidity that reflects trading volume in the underlying components of a fund. If a fund holds large and highly liquid stocks, it has good primary liquidity. Secondary liquidity shows the level of investor interest in an ETF: Are investors (particularly large institutions) actively buying and selling the ETF?

Liquidity, however, is not a constant. An ETF can see a sudden increase in activity, or it can fall off just as rapidly. For example, the Market Vectors Steel ETF (SLX) used to be a sleepy fund that traded only a few hundred shares a day. Then, in the summer of 2007, volume exploded. For the specialist in charge, this fund went from an extremely low-maintenance vehicle with low liquidity to a high-maintenance and liquid ETF. As Figure 5.1 shows, SLX, which tracks a very important basic materials sector, may see volume at or above one million shares, a far cry from where it started.

As an investor, you need to be aware of the factors that can affect liquidity, including global trends and industry developments. An ETF that follows a certain investment premise or theme may suddenly become attractive because of a change in an industry. Consider funds that focus on alternative energy sources, such as PowerShares WilderHill Clean Energy Portfolio (PBW), or Market Vectors Nuclear Energy ETF (NLR), which experienced a surge in volume in early 2010 based on renewed interest in nuclear power in the United States. Investors began looking for a nuclear revival after President Obama unveiled his 2011 budget that triples the amount of loan guarantees for nuclear power plants to $54 billion—receiving enthusiastic support from Democrats and Republicans alike.

Looking to capitalize on nuclear development, investors turned to NLR, which has heavy exposure to uranium mining firms that stand to see some of the largest gains as increased demand for nuclear energy drives up prices for crucial elements. The next largest portions of NLR

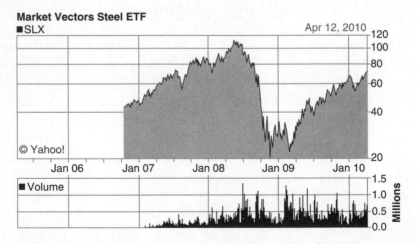

Figure 5.1 Volume in Market Vectors Steel (SLX) fund has expanded from its quiet beginnings in 2007.

are dedicated to nuclear power generation and the construction of nuclear plants. Also favoring this sector are technology developments on the horizon that could mean a shorter life span for waste, increased energy yield from available uranium, and the ability to recycle waste to further increase energy production. For investors looking for an energy revolution, NLR was a bright and shining idea (see Figure 5.2).

The green trend is also adding momentum to ETFs such as Barclays' iPath Global Carbon ETN (GRN). This fund is based on the Barclays Capital Global Carbon Index Total Return, which tracks two carbon-related credit plans: the European Union Emission Trading Scheme and the Kyoto Protocol's Clean Development Mechanism. GRN was a "first mover" in the U.S. carbon-emissions ETF space, which does give it somewhat of a strategic advantage. Admittedly, GRN's three-month average daily volume has been low, measuring less than 2,000 shares in early 2010; however, investor interest likely has been hampered by the fund's structure and limited scope. The inclusion of additional carbon-credit plans, which GRN managers anticipate, could make the fund more viable with investors, particularly as U.S. awareness of carbon-emissions plans increases. Although

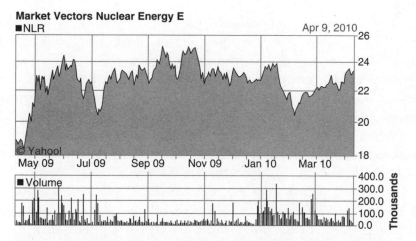

Figure 5.2 Market Vectors Nuclear Energy ETF (NLR) enjoyed increased volume in early 2010 based on the resurgence of interest in nuclear energy.
Source: Reproduced with permission of Yahoo! Inc. © 2010 Yahoo! Inc. YAHOO! and the YAHOO! logo are registered trademarks of Yahoo! Inc.

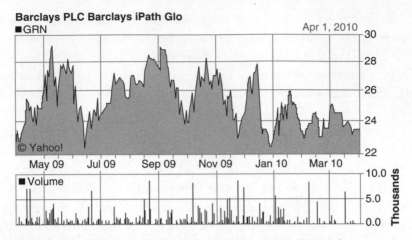

Figure 5.3 Barclays' iPath Global Carbon ETN (GRN) has seen spikes in volume, but increased liquidity would likely be needed to attract more investor interest.

GRN has seen several spikes in volume, as Figure 5.3 illustrates, a sustained increase in liquidity could very well draw further investor interest.

The point is whatever the emerging trend or change in an industry, these developments can boost certain funds that are suddenly thrust into the spotlight of investor attention. Some ETFs may be designed and launched at a moment in time when there isn't a great deal of demand for them. However, a certain event or development sparks interest by traders, which then favorably impacts liquidity.

When it comes to liquidity, you need to take two factors into consideration. The first is liquidity in the moment. For this, as previously stated, you will need to consider the average daily volume over a three-month period—not the previous day's volume. Liquidity has to be proven over time. Consistency in volume, and not just a spike on a single day, is what you want to see. Focus on funds that have a steady stream of liquidity, not those that are acting like a faucet that is being turned on and off.

The second factor is the prospect for a fund's liquidity in the future. Specifically, you should be on the lookout for developments that could cause a change in investor interest. For example, the launch of a lower-priced copycat product with lower fees could cause a decrease in trading volume for another ETF that was the first in an investment niche or sector. On the other hand, a favorable global trend could spark greater interest on a consistent and sustained basis.

You don't have to be a trained market analyst. As an ETF investor, you can intuitively figure out what is behind the liquidity in a fund and detect changes that could impact trading volume. Moreover, engaging in the thought process is empowering. What do you know or what have you read that could give you insight into inflation or economic growth? Is there a change in a political situation—becoming more or less stable—that will affect a particular foreign market? Is a particular industry poised to benefit from a change in regulation? Ask yourself: What are the developments globally that are impacting a particular industry or sector? For example, are more countries likely to rely on nuclear power? Has China put a massive stimulus program in place and is becoming a major buyer of steel? Questions such as these can yield clues about what the liquidity of an ETF would be like in the future.

Evidence of global trends can be found in the news, including developments in legislation and regulation. These big-picture events are usually outside of the stock market so you won't likely read about them in the business section; instead, the news analyses on these topics can be found on page A-1. As an investor, you are looking for news that will "bring more people to the game" instead of sitting on the sidelines or avoiding an ETF altogether. The more people who are interested in the fund that you are buying, the better the liquidity will be for you. Make sure that the liquidity is sustainable, and not just in response to a one-time event, such as the "cash for clunkers" program that provided a significant, but short-term, boost for the auto industry.

The best type of global trend is one that is likely to be sustained and expanded over time. Consider, for example, an announcement in early 2010 by the International Monetary Fund (IMF) that India would be one of the first nations to recover from the worldwide economic downturn, and that conditions were favorable for India to raise interest rates slowly. This signaled that growth in India would likely remain robust, despite moves to combat inflation that, as of February 2010, was at a 13-month high.

Upon hearing this news, you might have become interested in finding an ETF to capture the growth potential in India. The question then would be how to best make that play. Would you buy an Asian fund or one more targeted on India, such as PowerShares India (PIN)? In order to make that decision, you would have to do some research on what was being said about other economies in Asia. As we observed in February 2010, investors seemed more confident about India than they did about China. When China raised reserve requirements for banks slightly and moved to rein in loose credit, local and world markets reacted negatively. But when the Central Bank of India told lenders to increase cash reserves in late January, PIN and another Indian ETF, Wisdom Tree Indian Earnings (EPI), saw a gain on the day as investors seemed more confident in the Indian economy's ability to grow without government stimulus.

Let's say your research led you to believe that the Indian economy was better prepared than China's to be weaned from government support. Further, you learned that India didn't have a real-estate bubble, nor was there much volatility-inducing speculation by foreign investors in its stock market. Your conclusion may be that efforts to reduce inflation through tighter credit would be healthy for India, and that stocks in its market would advance as inflation dropped. If so, then you might have been one of the investors who was attracted to PIN (see Figure 5.4).

On the other side of the equation, beware of trends that presage a downturn in liquidity, particularly when an opportunity is coming to an end. Take a life-cycle fund, for example. As you recall from Chapter 3, life-cycle funds offer automatic asset allocation, from more aggressive in the beginning to more conservative at the end—and all targeted at a specific date when the investor presumably will retire. Given that a life-cycle fund has an expiration date, you can be sure that as you get close to that time, liquidity is going to dry up—or at least dry up in one direction, with a dearth of buyers but a plethora of sellers. Being aware of those dynamics will help you to determine what the liquidity is likely to be in the future before you pick a fund.

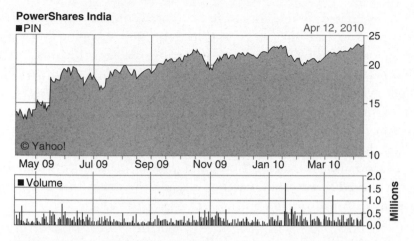

Figure 5.4 Improved economic growth prospects in India, as reported in late January 2010, resulted in increased volume for PowerShares India (PIN).

There are also developments in the ETF industry itself that could potentially affect liquidity in certain funds. For example, Fidelity Investments in February 2010 announced a partnership with iShares, offering Fidelity customers free access to 25 iShares domestic equity, international, and fixed income ETFs. As Fidelity explained, customers could use the funds to supplement an existing portfolio or to create an entire portfolio, without paying brokerage trading commissions.

If you were a Fidelity customer, that news probably would have interested you when it comes to your own trading and investing. But what if you were not a Fidelity customer? Why would you care? The fact is partnerships, alliances, and outright acquisitions that bring together investment companies and ETF issuers could potentially change the market dynamics. Think about it for a moment. A particular marketing alliance that greatly increases the volume of trading in particular ETFs could siphon off the liquidity in competing funds. As an investor in one fund or the other, you would want to be aware of such developments.

As we stated earlier, brokerage firms are trying to create a "stickier" customer base able to engage in "one-stop shopping," whether for mutual funds, ETFs, stocks, or other investments. Of course, there are other arguments to consider here, such as whether it really is good to get everything in one place. Competition in the ETF industry has led to greater innovation, lower fees, and greater transparency. If investment activity becomes more concentrated, could that actually impede liquidity in some products while benefiting others? Could this be a variation on the theme "too big to fail?" Whatever your opinion, watch the ETF industry for trends and new offerings that could add to potential opportunities and impact existing products.

When Newer Isn't Necessarily Better

Given the popularity of equity-based ETFs from the beginning, it stands to reason that issuers would try to offer as many variations as possible. As we have discussed, the new varieties include life-cycle ETFs and actively managed ETFs, just to name two. Every industry has its fads, and exchange-traded products are certainly no different. Just because a product is new, however, doesn't automatically mean that it's better. Sometimes even the most promising product fails to gain traction or live up to its potential. Exchange-traded notes (ETNs) are a perfect example.

ETNs were once heralded as the next great exchange-traded product. ETNs were first offered as a cost-effective means of gaining exposure to hard-to-access regions of the market such as commodities. Like exchange-traded funds, ETNs are designed to track specific benchmarks and trade on exchanges. That's where the similarities end. An ETF represents ownership in a portfolio of securities. An ETN represents exposure to an unsecured, unsubordinated debt obligation issued by a financial institution, such as Barclays, Deutsche Bank, or Credit Suisse. Like bonds, ETNs give investors a cash payment upon maturity. For ETNs, the payment is linked to how this instrument performs over its life span.

The ETN claim to fame has been the fact that they have virtually no tracking error, which was touted as an advantage over ETFs. Since

ETNs represent a debt agreement between issuer and investor, there is little or no tracking error if the fund is bought near its underlying value and held until maturity. ETNs also benefit from preferable tax treatments for notes.

When ETNs first appeared in 2006, investors rushed to invest in this next generation of exchange-traded products. For example, the iPath Dow Jones-UBS Commodity Index Total Return ETN (DJP) was launched in 2006 as an innovative way to add exposure to a wide range of commodities in a single investment. By August 2008, DJP's net assets reached $3.1 billion. By the summer of 2009, however, its net assets would fall by half. To understand what has happened to ETNs, we need to look back to their beginnings.

When ETNs were first being introduced, they attracted quite a lot of interest in the trading community as people tried to figure out how pricing would work. On the face of it, pricing seemed pretty straight-forward. ETNs are based on notes that expire somewhere in the future. Since every trade has two sides, as long as there were buyers and sellers, the ETN would literally track what it was supposed to track. The only question, which seemed obvious at the time (although, surprisingly, many people didn't see it this way), was the issue of credit risk. An ETN was only as good as the institution backing it.

The credit risk issue came home to roost when the global financial crisis hit. In 2008–2009, even banks that were sound were being looked at askance. The first domino to fall was Bear Stearns. On the brink of collapse in March 2008, it was taken over by JPMorgan Chase in a deal facilitated by the Federal Reserve and the Treasury Department. The move was a lucky one for investors in one particular Bear Stearns ETN fund. JPMorgan decided to keep the fund and change the name. Today it is known as the JPMorgan Alerian MLP Index ETN (AMJ).

Other funds suffered a different fate. According to the National Stock Exchange, the total number of listed ETNs decreased from 90 in October 2008 to 84 in October 2009. As of October 31, 2009, only $7.6 billion was invested in ETNs, compared with $699 billion invested in ETFs.

The hope and hype of the ETN market was apparent on a visit to Lehman Brothers in the late summer of 2008. Lehman had teams of four working on its ETN products, tasked with investment, marketing to clients, trading, and administration. Optimism for the new offerings was high at Lehman because many felt the absence of a tracking error would appeal strongly to investors. Just a few weeks after that visit, Lehman Brothers folded. As for the ETNs and other Lehman investment products, some of them were rebranded with the Barclays name, after Barclays took over some of the Lehman operations. And some of the Lehman products were closed.

The short history of ETNs has been marked by many failures and mishaps. One example is the iPath MSCI India Index ETN (INP), which has seen massive dislocations between its trading price and underlying value. By early 2010, India had once again capped the size of this fund due to its debt structure. As a result, in the month ending March 19, investors in INP saw the market value of their shares increase by only 7.55 percent, even though the underlying value of the index increased by more than 10.5 percent. Another ETN that has run into troubles, as we'll discuss in Chapter 7, is iPath Dow Jones-UBS Platinum Subindex Total Return^{SM} ETN. In early 2010, iPath also halted share creation in this platinum ETN because of concerns over futures trading position limits.

By the end of the first quarter of 2010, question marks began to appear over yet another ETN, this time the Credit Suisse Long/Short Liquid Index ETN (CSLS), which began trading in February. CSLS does *not* track the Credit Suisse Tremont Long/Short Equity Hedge Fund Index, as its name implies. Nor is CSLS a hedge fund ETN, as the "long/short" label might lead some to believe. It is an ETN that is backed by the creditworthiness of Credit Suisse.

The problem is that Credit Suisse has a poor track record in ETNs. In February 2009, it suspended creation/redemption for its gold ETN, and a bubble quickly formed, with the fund trading at a 1,000 percent premium. Even worse, in April 2009, Credit Suisse delisted three ETNs but did not liquidate the assets, leaving investors in exchange-traded limbo. Their investments traded over the counter, but they could only sell far below fair value. CSLS appears to be a fund with an uncertain future. Given all the possible outcomes—highly illiquid trading, share-creation suspension, delisting without liquidation—why would an investor choose to get involved? There are plenty of other candidates to consider. (In Chapter 7, we will look at the more honorable route that fund issuers can take when an ETN is shut down.)

Big Picture and Short-Term View

As you trade ETFs, remember what has made certain funds so successful in the past: good liquidity and closely tracking their NAV. These funds are typically based on something tangible, and not just a hypothesis or idea. Since transparency is a key attribute of ETFs, you want to buy funds that are consistent with their strategies, have a clearly worded and easily understood investment objective, and are based on a premise that you can count on.

In other trading venues such as stocks, investors often talk about finding a "hidden opportunity" that is not being widely followed. Traders often scour the market for these relatively unknown securities, believing that a positive event such as an upside earnings surprise could cause the share price to rocket. When that happens, they want to be onboard!

This is the exact opposite of the approach you want to take with ETFs. There is no glory in finding the undiscovered fund. Unless a fund has attracted strong investment interest and has good liquidity, its price will not be aligned with the NAV, and you will run the risk of paying an inflated price and selling at a depreciated one because the market maker needs to keep the spread wide in order to hedge an illiquid fund that may be holding thinly traded securities. ETFs that do not amass a strong holding also run a higher risk of sitting dead in the water or, worse yet, being terminated.

Even with a popular fund that is well followed, you need to know when to trade and when to stay on the sidelines. In other words, while it's essential that you understand the big picture—what a fund is based upon, how and where it trades, and what might make a fund more/less attractive in the foreseeable future—you can't forget the shorter-term view. This brings us back to the opening of this chapter, with the dynamics of the marketplace and all the nuances that make certain days and times more favorable to trade.

For example, after the three-day Presidents Day Weekend in February 2010, you may have been eager to trade when the market reopened on February 16. But if you had decided to trade, say, Market Vectors Small-Cap Brazil (BRF) or iShares FTSE/Xinhua China 25 Index ETF (FXI), you might have wished that you had taken another day off. The reason? The Hong Kong Stock Exchange was closed on February 16, 2010, for the Chinese New Year. As for Brazil, the market was closed on the same day to celebrate Carnival.

Keep in mind that the two ETFs, BRF and FXI, were open and trading on February 16 with no disruption, which could have caught investors unaware. But if you had done your homework, you would have known that the markets in which the underlying securities of the two ETFs trade were closed. Thus, you would realize that the only forces affecting those ETFs that day were the activities of the market makers. As we know from the discussion earlier in this chapter, that could have meant a considerable discrepancy between the price of the fund and its NAV. Instead, if you wanted to buy or sell shares of BRF or FXI, you would have been wise to wait until later in the week.

As this example shows, savvy ETF investors trade based on several factors. They pick sectors that have attracted investor interest and are likely to be even more popular in the foreseeable future. They focus on funds that have good liquidity, both in the ETF itself and in its underlying components. After they've made their choices, they enter the market prudently, knowing when to trade and when to sit on the sidelines and wait.

Chapter 6

International Investing

In 1519, Ferdinand Magellan embarked on an ambitious quest: circumnavigating the globe. In 1522, his expedition returned triumphantly to Spain, although the explorer himself was killed in a battle on an island in the Pacific. The world that had seemed so vast and unknowable suddenly became smaller, more manageable, and connected by trade. Today, world economies are interconnected, with multinational companies spanning several continents and global financial markets that trade virtually around the clock. Yet despite the trend toward greater globalization, which has made doing business in São Paulo not all that different from Singapore or San Francisco, there are opportunities to be reaped internationally—particularly in individual countries.

International investing is an effective way to diversify your equity holdings. As you weigh various opportunities, you should pay particular attention to developing markets that have less correlation with the United States than more developed economies. This lack of correlation offers you the potential to reap big returns from some international

ETFs, outpacing the major domestic benchmarks such as the S&P 500 or the NASDAQ. Consider iShares MSCI Brazil Index Fund (EWZ), which posted a return for 2009 of 124.46 percent as Brazil experienced economic growth and recovery bolstered by its energy industry. One-year returns do not mean that this fund—or the Brazilian economy, for that matter—will repeat that same performance this year or at any point in the future. What it illustrates, however, is the potential for explosive growth in certain international markets as recovery from the global economic crisis continues. If you are willing to stay on the alert for opportunities as they arise, as well as trouble that might surface suddenly, you can invest actively in geographic regions and single markets.

Gaining Exposure through Regional Funds

The amount of international exposure that's right for you depends upon your risk tolerance and your level of involvement. If you want to take a more hands-off approach, you are better off with a broad-based international equity fund that provides exposure across several countries. For a more active approach, you can pursue a single-market ETF, as long as you are willing to track your investment on a daily basis.

Overall, your international equity holdings will most likely be a mixture of both developing and emerging markets. Although emerging markets have gained a lot of attention lately, don't forget to include strong developed market funds in your portfolio to capture a mix of economies. Through one ETF you can gain exposure to several European economies as well as major companies that are domiciled in Europe. Since most international equity funds are weighted by market capitalization, you will gain access to the largest European companies. For example, Vanguard European ETF (VGK) tracks an index of companies located in the major markets of Europe. As Table 6.1 shows, about one-third of the fund's holdings in January 2010 were companies based in the United Kingdom.

Another fund in this space is the SPDR DJ Euro Stoxx 50 ETF (FEZ), which had more than a third of its holdings in France, as shown in Table 6.2.

Table 6.1 Country diversification for Vanguard
European ETF (VGK), as of January 31, 2010

Country	Percentage of Fund
United Kingdom	31.7%
France	16.3%
Germany	11.8%
Switzerland	11.7%
Spain	6.5%

SOURCE: Vanguard.com.

You can take a similar broad-based approach to emerging markets with ETFs that focus on multiple countries across one or several regions. For example, iShares MSCI Emerging Markets ETF (EEM) targets several emerging markets, including (as of January 31, 2010) Brazil (accounting for 13.95 percent of the fund's holdings), South Korea (13.23 percent), Taiwan (10.62 percent), China (10.41 percent), and South Africa (8.04 percent), followed by Hong Kong, Russia, India, Mexico, Israel, and others. A similar fund is Vanguard's Emerging Markets ETF (VWO) with top holdings (as of January 2010) of China (17.6 percent), Brazil (16.1 percent), South Korea (12.9 percent), Taiwan (11.1 percent), and India (7.7 percent), followed by Russia, South Africa, Mexico, Israel, and others.

For a somewhat more focused strategy, investors can take the well-known BRIC approach that targets the combination of Brazil, Russia, India, and China, which has long been the gold standard of emerging-market investing. This brings to mind BRIC funds such as iShares MSCI BRIC (BKF), Claymore/BNY Mellon BRIC (EEB),

Table 6.2 Country diversification for SPDR DJ
Euro Stoxx 50 ETF (FEZ), as of February 25, 2010

Country	Percentage of Fund
France	37.89%
Germany	26.22%
Spain	14.57%
Italy	10.54%

SOURCE: SPDRS.com.

Table 6.3   A comparison of the top country exposures for three BRIC ETFs

	iShares MSCI BRIC (BKF)	Claymore/BNY (EEB)	SPDR S&P BRIC 40 (BIK)
TOP 1 HOLDING	Brazil 33.57%	Brazil 56.85%	China 43.37%
TOP 2 HOLDING	China 22.43%	China 29.09%	Brazil 26.98%
TOP 3 HOLDING	India 14.65%	India 11.10%	Russia 21.90%
TOP 4 HOLDING	Russia 14.57%	Russia 2.96%	India 7.74%
	(as of Jan. 29, 2010)	(as of Dec. 31, 2009)	(as of Feb. 25, 2010)

SOURCE: iShares, Claymore, and SPDR.

and SPDR S&P BRIC 40 (BIK). Although these funds target the same countries, each takes a slightly different approach, as Table 6.3 shows.

Although trading BRIC ETFs remains popular, risk-tolerant investors have been taking more of an active, hands-on approach, seeking out the newest emerging-market ETF opportunities with funds that focus on individual countries such as Russia, Vietnam, Thailand, Turkey, and South Korea. Before jumping into a single-country strategy, however, you need to be aware of some serious potential downfalls as well as the promise for strong returns.

Single-Country Promise and Pitfalls

For more active investors, single-country ETFs are appealing as ways to pursue opportunities in both developed and developing markets. With this approach you will be able to cherry-pick your exposure country by country. For example, among developed economies, you might want to invest in Japan through a fund such as iShares MSCI Japan Index Fund (EWJ) fund. For European country exposure, iShares also has a number of offerings; for example, if you wanted to invest in Germany, there is iShares MSCI Germany Index Fund (EWG).

As you add single-country exposure to your portfolio, be mindful of the potential for overlap if you also hold a regional ETF. As you recall from earlier chapters, overlap occurs when a broader-based fund includes exposure to a particular sector or market, which is then increased by a more targeted ETF: for example, holding the technology-dominated QQQQ, which tracks the NASDAQ, as well as a technology ETF. The same concept applies with international investing. Let's say you owned Vanguard's Europe ETF VGK. You would want to know that nearly 12 percent of the fund's holdings are in Germany before you added a narrow ETF such as iShares MSCI Germany Index Fund (EWG).

Overlap is not the only concern when it comes to single-country investing. The more targeted the approach, the more carefully you have to watch for sudden developments that could turn a potential growth story into a worrisome scenario. For example, in February 2010, economic problems in Greece captured the headlines because of fears that the country could default on its debt payments. Although the news focused on Greece, investors also looked for other potential trouble spots in Europe, which put Italy in the crosshairs. At the national level and similar to Greece, Italy had used currency swaps to help it enter into the euro common currency. Although Italy was not in the same fiscal situation as Greece, investors found the parallel disconcerting. In response, iShares MSCI Italy (EWI) came under pressure. In February 2010, it was the second-worst performing Europe ETF for the previous three months (see Figure 6.1). Only iShares MSCI Spain (EWP), where the Spanish housing and banking situation had caused investor consternation, fared worse.

Going forward, the prognosis for the Italy fund (EWI) and the Spain fund (EWP) was that they would most likely be the most volatile among their European single-country counterparts. The concern was that should Greece fall, one or the other could become the next troubled nation at the center of global attention. That could also weaken the euro further, dragging down the value of all European assets. Even as the European Union's plan to bail out Greece was unveiled, investors remained watchful.

Not all the turbulence that can hit an ETF is financial-related. Consider what happened with iShares MSCI Turkey Invest Market Index (TUR), which began trading downward in late February 2010 because of mounting tensions between the Turkish government and military that led to a failed coup attempt. Suddenly this ETF, which

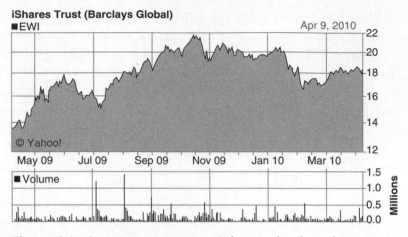

Figure 6.1 Investor concerns over Italy caused a sharp downturn in price of iShares MSCI Italy (EWI) in early 2010.
SOURCE: Reproduced with permission of Yahoo! Inc. © 2010 Yahoo! Inc. YAHOO! and the YAHOO! logo are registered trademarks of Yahoo! Inc.

had grown by more than 100 percent in 2009, saw a sharp price drop because of fears of political unrest (see Figure 6.2).

What's important to understand here was that Turkey's long-term prospects for economic growth remained strong, although there had been some concern over short-term weakness in exports. The trigger

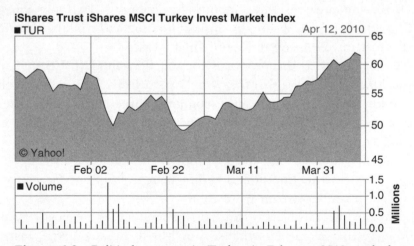

Figure 6.2 Political concerns in Turkey in February 2010 sparked a sharp sell-off in iShares MSCI Turkey Invest Market Index (TUR), from approximately $58 a share to below $48 within a few weeks.
SOURCE: Reproduced with permission of Yahoo! Inc. © 2010 Yahoo! Inc. YAHOO! and the YAHOO! logo are registered trademarks of Yahoo! Inc.

for the sell-off was purely political. The lesson here is when you invest in hopes of capturing a strong growth story, you must keep your eyes open for any development that could derail your investment plans. As we stated in Chapter 5, that means reading the front section of the newspaper and not just the business pages.

Although the examples of market turmoil in Greece, Italy, and Turkey are sobering, they should not discourage you from exploring the potential of international investing as long as you remain very aware. As you will see in the next examples, strong economic growth and prospects for future expansion are fueling investor interest in a variety of emerging markets.

By the end of 2009, Brazil had emerged from the global economic crisis with a stronger financial system and a positive outlook. Much of Brazil's success was being pegged on the continuing recovery of the commodity markets. Favorable developments that also drew investor attention were formidable steps taken by the Brazilian government to renew the country's financial system and eagerness among countries around the globe to invest in a country that is so rich in commodities.

The strength of Brazil's economic story can be seen in a single-country fund such as iShares MSCI Brazil Index Fund (EWZ), which as previously noted posted a return for 2009 of 124.46 percent. EWZ is the largest and most liquid of the Brazil ETFs. The fund, founded in 2000, is also the most time-tested of the bunch. The index it tracks contains 67 Brazilian companies that trade primarily on the Bolsa de Valores de Saulo. One thing to note is that EWZ is market cap–weighted. Two different shares of energy giant Petrobras make up the top two holdings of the fund, accounting for about 21 percent. As an investor you should be aware of such concentration in one company and one industry.

Another Brazil-specific fund is Market Vectors Brazil Small Cap (BRF), which was launched in May 2009 to offer investors access to smaller companies in Brazil that should benefit from an increasing consumer base and a growing middle class. This fund targets small-cap companies that are domiciled and primarily listed on an exchange in Brazil or that generate at least 50 percent of their revenues in Brazil. As Figure 6.3 illustrates, the strength of the Brazilian economy sent BRF prices skyrocketing—doubling between late May and December 2009.

Figure 6.3   A chart of Market Vectors Brazil Small-Cap (BRF) shows a rapid rise in the price of the fund during the second half of 2009.

Source: Reproduced with permission of Yahoo! Inc. © 2010 Yahoo! Inc. YAHOO! and the YAHOO! logo are registered trademarks of Yahoo! Inc.

Although BRF offers a pure play on Brazil's economy over time, you must be aware of the volatility that comes with a portfolio of small-cap stocks. This is yet another reminder that you cannot rely upon an ETF's name alone. You need to investigate its investment theme and how it carries out that premise.

Another attractive market in 2009 was Mexico as the country navigated the global downturn better than expected. The promise of this market was evident in iShares MSCI Mexico Investable Market Index Fund (EWW), which posted total returns for 2009 of 55.72 percent. Not only did EWW hold up longer than other foreign exchange-traded funds in 2008, it recovered just as quickly—thanks to the country's diversified trade (see Figure 6.4). Although the United States remains Mexico's most important trade partner, it increased exports to other nations in recent years. Trade with Costa Rica, Chile, Honduras, and the European Union has grown rapidly.

Further cushioning Mexico has been its extensive access to commodities, especially oil. Mexico is the third-largest supplier of oil to the United States and is the world's tenth-largest crude producer.

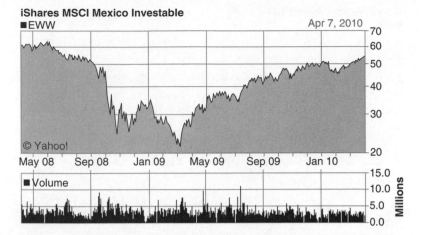

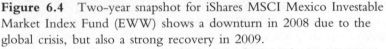

Figure 6.4 Two-year snapshot for iShares MSCI Mexico Investable Market Index Fund (EWW) shows a downturn in 2008 due to the global crisis, but also a strong recovery in 2009.
Source: Reproduced with permission of Yahoo! Inc. © 2010 Yahoo! Inc. YAHOO! and the YAHOO! logo are registered trademarks of Yahoo! Inc.

Given Mexico's other exports of silver, copper, fruits, coffee, cotton, and other major commodities, strengthening prices helped Mexico insulate itself from a troubled U.S. economy in 2009.

Single-country funds are usually pursued opportunistically, when the growth story in a specific market looks appealing, such as Russia in 2009. Market Vectors Russia (RSX) is composed of publicly traded companies that are domiciled in Russia and traded in Russia and/or on leading global exchanges. RSX offered a pure play in Russia, posting a strong return, particularly from March 2009 through January 2010, as shown in Figure 6.5. Much of that growth was due to the strength of the energy industry, which is strongly represented in RSX.

Commodity Plays

In 2009, the story in Russia was energy. In the second quarter of 2009, while OPEC nations were undertaking production cuts, Russia

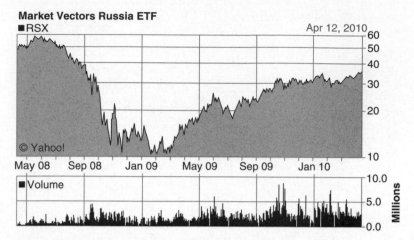

Figure 6.5   The price of Market Vectors Russia (RSX) more than tripled from March 2009 through early 2010.
SOURCE: Reproduced with permission of Yahoo! Inc. © 2010 Yahoo! Inc. YAHOO! and the YAHOO! logo are registered trademarks of Yahoo! Inc.

surpassed Saudi Arabia in crude oil production. RSX was seen as a good play for investors who wanted to tap Russia's oil opportunities. Although Market Vectors says its RSX fund has less emphasis on energy than do competing indexes and funds, the oil and gas sector still dominates this ETF. Four of the five top holdings in RSX, as of February 26, 2010, were energy companies Gazprom (7.93 percent), Lukoil (7.76 percent), Rosneft Oil (7.56 percent), and Surgutneftegaz (5.81 percent). Another top holding was financial firm Sberbank (7.91 percent).

As you can see, international funds, particularly those in developing markets, can double as commodity plays if a significant portion of a country's economy is derived from a natural resource. Although this can work to an investor's advantage, it pays to be aware of what is driving the economic growth in a country. For example, if you held RSX, you would want to know that it was heavily invested in energy, particularly if you also owned oil sector funds.

The inverse can also be true. An ETF that focuses on commodities can offer you exposure to a unique international market in which it otherwise would be difficult to participate. Consider two new ETFs that are physically backed by two of the most expensive precious metals, platinum and palladium. ETFS Physical Platinum Shares (PPLT) and ETFS Physical Palladium Shares (PALL) were launched in early 2010. These funds appealed strongly to investors looking for exposure to precious metals beyond silver and gold.

In the past, investors who wanted exposure to the platinum market had to rely on flawed, futures-backed offerings such as iPath Dow Jones-UBS Platinum Subindex Total Return ETN (PGM), which at times has traded out of sync with its net asset value. The problem with PGM was that growth of the fund could potentially impact the thin market for platinum futures and lead to suspension of creation of new shares, which has happened in the past.

No such problem exists for ETFS Physical Platinum Shares (PPLT). Now, investors are able to gain exposure to physical platinum without bearing the expense of buying a bar of the metal. For ETF investors seeking access to the palladium market, PALL is the first such opportunity among ETFs.

The appeal of these two precious metals is not all glitter. Both platinum and palladium are backed by a strong economic story. Platinum and palladium prices have been helped by increasing demand from the global auto industry, which uses the metals in catalytic converters. Now, as more consumers in China buy cars, some observers are raising the possibility that the global green trend and the push for cleaner emissions might translate into a boom for catalytic converters in China.

For ETF investors, PPLT and PALL are more than just a commodity play. The funds also offer a gateway to the South African economy, which would be difficult to access otherwise. Some 80 percent of the world's platinum production comes from South Africa, which is also a major palladium producer. Therefore, by investing in these funds, you gain not only exposure to the physical metals themselves, but also economic exposure in a unique corner of the world.

This is yet another example of thinking outside the proverbial box when it comes to international investing. You need to consider not only the facts at hand, but also other undercurrents that might be impacting a fund, making it more or less attractive as an investment.

ADRs versus Ordinaries

As you explore international equity exposure, you will encounter the choice of American Depositary Receipts (ADRs) versus ordinaries. Both types of securities have their advantages and their drawbacks. ADRs are dollar-denominated instruments that trade in U.S. equity markets and allow investors to buy and sell stakes in foreign companies. For example, the ADR for Finland's Nokia Corp. trades on the New York Stock Exchange under the symbol NOK. By buying the ADR you own a stake in the foreign company without having to trade on a non-U.S. exchange. This makes ADRs less complicated for U.S. investors, and there are ETFs that seek to replicate international exposure with ADRs. For example, BLDRS Emerging Markets 50 ADR Index (ADRE) tracks an index of 50 ADRs of the most actively traded companies in international and emerging markets. The fund's top country allocations, as of February 26, 2010, were Brazil, China, and South Korea, even though the securities it holds are traded in the United States.

With ADRs, however, you are a step away from the international market. You are not holding the primary shares, but rather a product that has been created for the U.S. market. In addition, because ADRs are denominated in dollars and traded on a U.S. exchange, there is a currency component to pricing. The biggest drawback, however, is the limited number of ADRs trading on U.S. exchanges compared to the entire universe of foreign equities trading in their home markets and on global exchanges.

If you want to trade ETFs that hold foreign equities, there are issues to consider here as well. One of the biggest concerns is investment restrictions that may be placed on U.S. and other "foreign" investors in overseas markets. These restrictions can negatively impact the trading and growth of an ETF. As you recall from earlier discussions, as an ETF grows, more shares are created. In the case of an international equity ETF, the new shares are based on securities that trade overseas. Any restrictions that are placed on the amount of the underlying securities that can be owned by outside investors will limit the growth of the ETF.

Such restrictions became an issue for iPath MSCI India Index ETN (INP). As an ETN, this exchange-traded product was based on debt instruments, not equities. Nonetheless, the example aptly illustrates the problem. In late 2009, creation of new shares in INP was suspended after the Securities and Exchange Board of India (SEBI) alleged that the fund issuer had not complied with reporting requirements involving its derivative-based products. Specifically, SEBI expressed concern over how foreigners access India's equity market. Rather than tracking a basket of Indian equities, INP's portfolio, which is comprised of unsubordinated debt securities, is designed to track the performance of the Indian equity market. The suspension for INP was part of a larger and ongoing regulatory battle over derivative-based exchange-traded products and concerns over foreign investments in emerging markets. When it comes to India and INP, we should note that investment restrictions affect derivative-based India funds, not India funds as a whole. Trading has been normal in PowerShares India (PIN) and WisdomTree India Earnings (EPI) ETFs, which track baskets of India securities. As a result, these equity-based ETFs are more stable ways to access India's market as regulatory issues around derivative-based exchange traded instruments are resolved.

India is not the only country that has expressed concern over the rapid influx of overseas investors in its markets. Similar apprehension has been voiced by China, and Brazilian authorities instituted a 2 percent tax on Brazilian stocks that trade as ADRs. Knowing this, your best strategy is to look for international funds that track baskets of ordinary stocks trading in foreign markets. Look for funds that are well established, frequently traded, and liquid. At all times keep your eyes open for economic and geopolitical developments that could impact your holdings, whether promising a new opportunity or warning of a troublesome scenario.

Shifting Targets

A market is hot, and then it is not. Therefore, the investment opportunities you pursue in a single country, particularly those in emerging markets, are often reaped over a period of months. These are not "buy and hold" investments for an autopilot type of investor. They require close monitoring on a daily basis. There are times, however, when you must be patient for an opportunity to set up as you test the waters with a small position. For example, iShares MSCI Thailand Investable Market Index (THD) and iShares MSCI Taiwan Index (EWT) showed strong appeal early in 2010 because of their exposure to rapidly growing markets in Asia. The two funds, which are highly liquid, attracted investors who were looking for an Asian growth story outside of China.

Another enticing opportunity for risk-tolerant investors is Vietnam, where, despite a fall in exports, the economy continued to gain momentum propelled by domestic growth. Highlighting continued investor interest, in the second half of 2009 Van Eck Global launched Market Vectors Vietnam (VNM), which invests in the 30 largest companies in and around Vietnam (see Figure 6.6). Vietnam's business-friendly attitude and workforce continue to be viewed as positive factors supporting the ETF, and more recent developments have

Figure 6.6 A six-month snapshot of Van Eck Global–launched Market Vectors Vietnam (VNM) shows price volatility and thin volume. Nonetheless, some observers see potential in this growing Asian market.

Source: Reproduced with permission of Yahoo! Inc. © 2010 Yahoo! Inc. YAHOO! and the YAHOO! logo are registered trademarks of Yahoo! Inc.

further increased the potential. A large government stimulus package helped to increase consumer demand, propel property prices, and bolster businesses.

Despite the promise of the upside, Vietnam's marketplace is still small, and foreigners may face difficulty investing because of capital controls. Only 40 companies in the market have a market cap over $200 million. Will the promise outweigh the potential pitfalls? Time will tell. However, the signs are promising. For example, international manufacturers that had been operating in China are looking at Vietnam, particularly as production costs in China rise. In fact, some observers say Vietnam looks very much like China did a decade ago. That alone could be sufficient reason to get involved in this new ETF with a small stake.

New Offerings Ahead

If the recent past is any indication of the future, there will be no shortage of new offerings as fund issuers come up with innovative ways to target interesting investment premises and exotic markets. To cite just one example, Van Eck Global announced in mid-February 2010 the launch of the Market Vectors Egypt Index ETF (EGPT) as the first U.S.-based ETF to provide focused exposure to Egypt's economy. In its announcement, Van Eck touted Egypt's economic growth and its move to establish a more open, market-oriented economy that has led to expanding foreign investment, net exports, industrial development, and business formation.

A look at almost any major ETF issuer's web site will reveal new offerings in the international market, including emerging economies as well as international sectors. These new offerings allow you to participate in a particular sector—such as finance or basic materials—in a specific region of the world, including developed and developing markets. For example, in early 2010 iShares MSCI Emerging Markets Materials Sector Index Fund (EMMT) was launched along with iShares MSCI Europe Financial Sector Index (EUFN), iShares MSCI Emerging Markets Financial Sector Index Fund (EMFN), and iShares MSCI Far East Financial Sector Index Fund (FEFN).

With such explosive growth globally, the ETF industry has clearly moved out of its infancy into an adolescent phase: awkward, gangly, and a period that in 20 years we wish we could have avoided. During this time we'll continue to see products introduced faster than regulators can find ways to control them. Methodologies will bump up against regulations in products, affecting not only new entrants but also funds that are already trading. As we've stated all along, some funds will gain traction and a strong investor following and some will not. If you are willing to pursue the opportunities that lie before you, as well as those that are on the horizon, you could be in for quite an adventure in international investing.

Chapter 7

Gaining Exposure to Commodities

From the introduction of the first equity ETF, it was only a matter of time before these products expanded into virtually every conceivable market. Once investors discovered the ease of buying shares in an ETF, their appetites were whetted for other investment vehicles that could give them access to sectors and markets in which they previously had not been able to participate easily.

The commodities market is certainly an apt example. As we have seen recently, demand for commodity exposure through ETFs has exploded and shows little sign of abating. In the commodity space, there are four basic ways to gain exposure:

1. Physically backed funds
2. Equity funds
3. Futures-based funds
4. Exchange-traded notes (ETNs)

The array of strategies makes the commodities market a microcosm of the entire ETF industry. Highlighting the innovation of ETF issuers, physically backed funds have opened the door to stockpiles of gold, platinum, and palladium to retail investors. Commodity exposure can also be pursued through the traditional approach of equity-based ETFs: tracking baskets of stocks of companies involved in mining, production, and other commodity-related activities. Equity-based ETFs are not only familiar, but also provide transparency through baskets of stocks that you can easily identify and track. Futures-based funds mirror the riskier derivative approaches that have been cropping up in some ETFs. Although these products appear to be cutting-edge, new regulatory restrictions could make futures-based commodity funds less predictable and, therefore, less attractive for investors. Finally, ETNs were once touted as a highly promising product, but more recently have run into troubles because of credit risk. In addition, commodity ETNs face the same futures-trading restrictions as their ETF brethren.

As you can see, each of the four varieties has advantages and drawbacks. As you contemplate which fund is right for your portfolio, you need to be particularly discerning about a fund's objective and how it pursues that goal. Does the ETF hold the physical commodity, or does it use futures contracts to replicate exposure? Does it hold equities of companies that are engaged in the production of a particular commodity? Your investment decision needs to be based on far more than just the name of the ETF. Just because a fund's name includes "oil," "natural gas," "gold," and so on, you can't be sure how that fund accomplishes exposure to that particular commodity. In order to make the best choice to fit your portfolio, you must mine the options and see where and how you can pursue pay dirt.

Physical Commodity ETFs—Panning for Profits

Nothing has glittered like gold recently, trading well above $1,000 an ounce, and putting in a recent high over $1,200 in December 2009. Often viewed as a hedge against inflation and a "flight to quality" investment when other assets are under pressure, gold has traditionally been viewed as a safe haven during times of uncertainty.

Gold is also much more than an investment. The metal has been regarded as precious for millennia (consider King Tut's burial mask that was made of gold). Today, gold is considered to have special appeal because it is typically immune to factors that move the prices of everything from stocks to housing. If you are looking to gain exposure to gold, one tactic to consider is buying the physical metal—through an ETF, that is.

A visit to the web site for SPDR Gold Trust (GLD) (see http://www.spdrgoldshares.com) makes the point visually. A colored photo on the site shows gold bars stacked on pallets like so many building bricks. Investors who buy shares in this ETF are gaining an ownership stake in the fund's stockpile of gold bullion, without having to deal with physical delivery or with logistics such as storing and insuring physical gold. Other ETFs backed by bullion include iShares Comex Gold Trust (IAU) and ETFS Physical Swiss Gold Shares (SGOL). The prices of these ETFs rise or fall depending upon gold prices—in other words, how much people want to pay for physical gold. See Figure 7.1.

One caveat for investors who want access to physical gold is the tax implication. Unlike other ETFs, bullion-backed funds are taxed up to

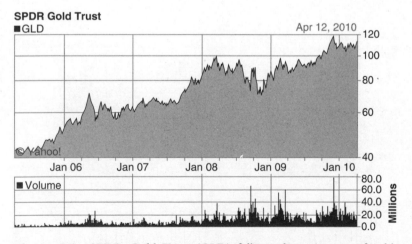

Figure 7.1 SPDR Gold Trust (GLD) follows the trajectory of gold prices as investors have sought exposure to the precious metal.
SOURCE: Reproduced with permission of Yahoo! Inc. © 2010 Yahoo! Inc. YAHOO! and the YAHOO! logo are registered trademarks of Yahoo! Inc.

25 percent as collectibles. Therefore, these funds are better suited for long-term investors looking to diversify a broader portfolio.

Investors can also use ETFs to gain exposure to physical silver through funds such as iShares Silver Trust (SLV) and ETFS Physical Silver Shares (SIVR). Among the most exciting newcomers among all ETFs are two funds launched in early 2010 by ETF Securities as part of a suite of four precious metals funds. In addition to its physical gold and silver products, ETF Securities offers funds that are backed by physical stockpiles of platinum and palladium. As mentioned in Chapter 6, ETFS Physical Platinum (PPLT) and ETFS Physical Palladium (PALL) could be used to gain indirect exposure to the South African economy. The real appeal of these two funds, however, is to obtain access to physical supplies of exotic precious metals.

Since their launch, PPLT and PALL have created quite a stir. In fact, there were reports early on that suggested that strong investor interest in these two physically backed funds may have boosted the prices of the metals they track. Figure 7.2 shows the price action in PPLT soon after the fund was launched in early 2010.

The sudden influx of funds into PPLT reveals just how eager investors have been to gain entry to what was previously off limits.

Figure 7.2   Price action in ETFS Physical Platinum (PPLT) tracks the platinum market.

Launched on January 8, 2010, PPLT amassed more than $430 million in assets in just two months. It was clear from the beginning that PPLT was superior to the only other platinum vehicle: iPath Dow Jones–UBS Platinum Subindex Total Return^{SM} ETN (PGM), which is an ETN that is based on futures contracts—not the physical metal. (We will discuss PGM's problems later in the chapter.)

With such a promising start, PPLT and PALL seemed poised in 2010 to ride a wave should platinum and palladium prices move higher. Prospects seem bright, given increasing demand for the two precious metals from the global auto industry. Increasing production costs in South Africa, which mines 80 percent of the world's platinum, could potentially lead to volume cutbacks that could boost prices even higher.

If you are looking for a pure play in commodities, funds that offer exposure to the physical metals are excellent candidates to consider, especially if you are taking a long-term position. The drawback, besides the tax implications for precious metals, is that there is a limited number of physically backed ETFs at this point. For exposure to other commodities, you will have to consider different investment options.

Equity-Based Commodity Exposure

Another way to gain exposure to commodities is through the companies that produce, transport, and store them. An equity-based commodity ETF offers "leverage-like" exposure to commodities through the stocks of companies involved in natural resources and other raw materials. These equity funds are viable alternatives to futures-backed ETFs, which may be subject to trading limits and other regulatory restrictions. Further, equity-based commodity ETFs have better tax implications than ETFs that hold physical stockpiles of precious metals.

For investors who want the familiarity of an ETF that tracks baskets of equities, these funds may be especially appealing. For example, the First Trust ISE-Revere Natural Gas Index Fund (FCG) tracks U.S. companies that are involved in the exploration and production of

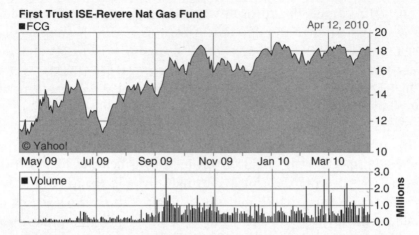

Figure 7.3   First Trust ISE-Revere Natural Gas Index Fund (FCG)
attracted investor volume as an alternative to futures-based natural gas
ETFs.
Source: Reproduced with permission of Yahoo! Inc. © 2010 Yahoo! Inc. YAHOO!
and the YAHOO! logo are registered trademarks of Yahoo! Inc.

natural gas (see Figure 7.3). For investors wanting to have exposure
to this important energy commodity, FCG is certainly a far better
candidate in our view than United States Natural Gas (UNG), which,
as we will discuss later in this chapter, has had to change its investment strategy because of regulatory limits on the number of futures
contracts it can hold.

Another example in the energy sector is iShares Dow Jones U.S.
Oil Equipment & Services Index Fund (IEZ). Although two companies, Schlumberger and Halliburton, constitute 20.6 percent and 10.2
percent respectively (as of March 2010), the market conditions that
these firms face are representative of the industry as a whole.

Other equity-based funds with exposure to commodities through
companies that produce, process, or transport them include Jefferies
CRB Commodity Equity Index Fund (CRBQ) and Market Vectors
RVE Hard Assets Producers Index Fund (HAP). As of March 2010,
the top three holdings of both funds were Exxon Mobil, Monsanto,
and Potash Corp. of Saskatchewan, although the weighting differed
slightly between the funds.

For investors looking to gain exposure to gold, there are equity-based alternatives such as Market Vectors Gold Miners (GDX) and Market Vectors Junior Gold Miners (GDXJ). GDX provides exposure to worldwide companies that are involved primarily in mining for gold, including large-, mid-, and small-cap stocks. GDXJ tracks small- and mid-cap companies involved in gold and/or silver mining. Among the two, GDX probably offers the most stability. As the fund issuer noted on its site, GDXJ's portfolio includes companies that may not have begun to generate material revenues and that may operate at a loss, which could contribute to greater volatility, lower trading volume, and less liquidity than larger companies.

One advantage of investing in funds such as GDX and GDXJ is that they are treated like stocks for tax purposes, unlike bullion-based funds that are taxed up to 25 percent as collectibles. This tax treatment makes these funds more suitable for short-term players in the gold market. However, mining companies that are located outside the United States could be affected by high fixed operating costs and currency issues, which could also impact the ETF. See Figure 7.4.

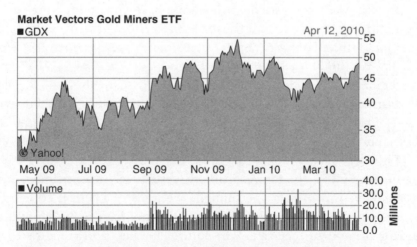

Figure 7.4 Volume numbers for Market Vectors Gold Miners (GDX) showed strong investor interest, particularly in the second half of 2009 and early 2010, as interest in gold continued.
SOURCE: Reproduced with permission of Yahoo! Inc. © 2010 Yahoo! Inc. YAHOO! and the YAHOO! logo are registered trademarks of Yahoo! Inc.

Beware the Futures-Backed Commodity Fund

To those who are unaware, it could appear to be a good idea. To pursue your desired exposure, you choose a fund with the targeted commodity right in its name. Let's use a hypothetical example: American Metal Fund, to which we'll give the symbol MTLL. As you read about the fund, you see that it is designed to track in percentage terms the movement of certain metal prices such as gold, silver, copper, and aluminum. So far, so good; after all, you're trying to get exposure to the prices of the underlying commodities.

The problem, however, is that you have not yet asked the question that, as an investor, you must always consider: How does the ETF pursue its objective? To find out, you must read further into the fund description or prospectus. As you investigate MTLL, you find the answer in the investment objective language. The fund seeks to reflect changes in percentage terms of the price of metals as reflected in the price of *futures contracts*. In MTLL's description of its portfolio, you read that the fund holds futures contracts, forward contracts, and swaps.

By this point, the warning bell should have gone off in your head. Increased regulatory pressure has made the performance of some funds that hold futures contracts nearly impossible to predict. Such has been the fate of funds such as United States Natural Gas (UNG) and PowerShares DB Commodity (DBC), which suddenly faced regulatory scrutiny after these ETFs proved to be too popular for their own good. That's right—too much investor interest created problems for these funds, as we'll explain in a moment.

First, let's take a look at the appeal of futures-based funds. Before commodity ETFs, the futures markets were largely inaccessible to the average investor. Even if you thought the price of a certain commodity was going to go up, you probably would not have opened a futures trading account to speculate. The futures market is an arena best left to experienced professionals.

When commodity ETFs were introduced, suddenly you could more easily access these investment opportunities. Now, just by buying shares in an ETF, you could get exposure to the spot price of a commodity, such as natural gas, crude oil, and so forth. The problem, however, is the way futures-based ETFs are created. As you recall, equity-based ETFs are created by exchanging shares of the companies that the fund tracks for shares of the ETFs. With a futures-based commodity ETF, however, shares are created by exchanging an appropriate number of futures contracts. The greater the demand for the futures-based ETF, the more contracts that have to be purchased.

For funds such as United States Natural Gas (UNG), the size of its futures positions became problematic on two fronts. First, because futures contracts expire, positions have to be rolled forward, meaning they are sold in the expiring month and purchased in the next month out. With so many contracts to sell in the front month and to purchase in the next month, UNG's rolling position exacerbated the price differential known as "contango." Contango in the futures market means the near-term price is lower than the next month's to reflect carrying charges. With UNG, the more it grew, the larger the contango became, which disrupted the futures market.

The size of UNG and other futures-based funds also attracted the attention of the Commodity Futures Trading Commission (CFTC). In the summer of 2009, the CFTC very noisily stepped in and voiced concern that the funds were influencing the very things they were supposed to track. When the CFTC began talking about the possibility of position limits, some of the larger futures-based commodity funds began to react. UNG, for example, announced it was not going to issue any additional shares, which resulted in the fund trading at a significant premium to its NAV.

When funds have to halt share creation, it's a serious situation. Without new shares to create, market makers cannot hedge their exposure. Therefore, spreads widen and huge premiums and discounts to the NAV can occur. A fund can't stay in share-creation limbo forever; something has to give. Funds have to choose between one of two basic choices: Change or close. As you'll read in a moment, UNG was among a few funds that chose the former.

In January 2010, after months of speculation, the CFTC set forth new proposals that would curb UNG and United States Oil (USO), as well as other funds. In fact, the CFTC cited both UNG and USO as examples to illustrate the necessity of its "Proposed Position Limit Rule." The new CFTC proposal covers futures contracts for natural gas, light sweet crude oil, heating oil, and gasoline blend-stock traded on the New York Mercantile Exchange (NYMEX) and the Intercontinental Exchange (ICE).

To keep from violating trading limits and to avoid regulatory action, UNG changed its investment strategy. The action was necessary because after share creation was halted, UNG traded at a huge premium. The only way to bring prices back in line with the fund's valuation was to create new shares backed by something other than futures contracts. UNG's investment alternative was swaps—an agreement between two parties based on underlying assets—which trade in the over-the-counter market. On its web site, UNG specifies that authorized purchasers wishing to participate in share creation must engage in natural gas–based swaps.

A similar development occurred in PowerShares DB Commodity Index Tracking Fund (DBC), which is composed of futures contracts on 14 of the most heavily traded and important physical commodities in the world, including crude oil, heating oil, gasoline, natural gas, gold, and silver. Facing an influx of investor interest, DBC also changed its strategy midstream to avoid regulatory issues related to its positions in the futures market. In fact, during its restructuring, DBC took the unusual step of exchanging some of its futures contracts traded on NYMEX for Brent oil futures contracts, which trade abroad.

By restructuring mid-strategy, these funds were allowed to resume or continue creating shares, which helped to bring fund prices back in line with their NAVs. However, it is hardly an ideal solution. When funds must change the way they create shares, they have materially changed their composition. For you, the investor, that means you are not getting exactly what you had bargained for when you bought the fund. You wanted exposure to the futures market, but now the shares you hold represent something else: over-the-counter swaps.

The growing pains experienced by UNG and DBC show just how young the ETF industry really is. As products are launched in new territory, there is no guarantee what will happen. As UNG and DBC raced ahead, fueled by the popularity of these investment products, they suddenly hit a wall of regulatory concern. As a result, the funds had to make an emergency pit stop in order to retool. The choice was clear: Adapt or die. Remember, the primary goal of ETF issuers is to attract assets by offering either innovative products or funds that have lower fees than competing offerings. In other words, a fund is either a first mover or it's a cheaper copycat. When fund issuers slam into a regulatory barrier, they need to find a way around the obstacle. They want to keep the door open so that assets can keep flowing in. Obviously, share creation halts do not accomplish that. The only way forward is to offer exposure to the underlying market through another means. In the case of futures-backed funds, that has meant turning increasingly to swaps, which are over-the-counter derivatives.

We hope that eventually regulators come to some elegant solution for futures-backed funds; for example, imposing limits in more thinly traded markets such as cotton or copper, while giving funds freer rein in larger and more liquid commodities such as natural gas and oil. At this point, however, such a solution is still wishful thinking on the part of the ETF industry. The reality right now is hardly elegant, but it works. Switching from futures to bilateral swaps for some of a fund's holdings is not a perfect solution, but in the face of regulatory restrictions and a bubble forming in the fund price, it was the best that could be done at the time.

Using ETNs to Gain Access to Commodities

The fourth way to gain access to commodities is by using ETNs, which as you recall are senior, unsubordinated, unsecured debt issued by an institution. ETNs are linked to a variety of assets, including commodities and currencies. ETNs are designed to have "no tracking error" between the product and its underlying index. Owners of an ETN such as iPath Dow Jones-AIG Commodity ETN (DJP) will get the return of the index, minus the management fees.

Commodity ETNs also offer a more favorable tax treatment over commodity ETFs. Investors who hold a commodity ETN for more than one year pay only a 15 percent capital gains tax when they sell a product. Futures-based commodity ETFs are taxed like futures, and gains are marked to market every year. This 23 percent versus 15 percent tax difference has helped attract investors to ETNs.

A wide variety of commodity ETNs are available, from those that track a single product to sector-specific and broader indexes. For example, the iPath family of ETNs includes those that track industrial metals such as aluminum, copper, lead, nickel, and tin; "soft" commodities such as cocoa, coffee, cotton, and sugar; and energy commodities such as natural gas and oil. Sector ETNs offer exposure to energy, agriculture, grains, soft commodities, industrial metals, precious metals, and livestock, as well as broader index products. As with any exchange-traded product, a narrower focus—for example, an ETN based on a single commodity as opposed to a sector or a diversified basket of commodities—could make liquidity an issue.

With so many advantages, especially the tax treatment of commodity ETNs, why isn't this category booming? As we discussed in Chapter 5, one of the concerns about ETN is credit risk of the issuing bank. Post-financial crisis it isn't so hard to imagine bank failures that, not that long ago, would have seemed to be a rare, once-in-a-century occurrence. On top of the credit risk, ETNs that track futures also have regulatory risk. Just as we saw with futures-backed ETFs such as UNG, regulatory restrictions on a fund's involvement in the futures market can also impact an ETN.

Consider what has happened with iPath Dow Jones–UBS Platinum Subindex Total Return ETN (PGM), which is based on platinum futures contracts. The platinum futures market, unlike that for natural gas or crude oil, is very thinly traded. When PGM grew because of investor interest, this ETN suddenly became a large participant in a small market. Given the CFTC's wariness of funds having too much influence over the commodity markets they are supposed to track, PGM soon became subject to new futures safety limits.

Regulatory concerns barred PGM from creating any more shares because it could not acquire more platinum futures contracts. That, in turn, disrupted the ETN's share-pricing process, as the notes began to lag their underlying index. In late 2009, iPath issued a news release warning investors that suspension of share creation could cause "fluctuations in trading value" of PGM. That was an understatement. As Figure 7.5 shows, PGM quickly ramped up to a premium over its underlying value.

The original strategy of PGM was interrupted by futures safety limits. A primary tenet of the ETF industry is transparent exposure to

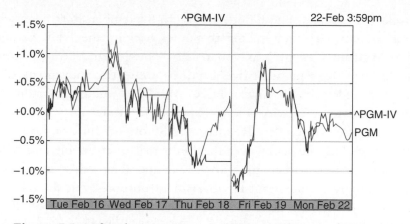

Figure 7.5 After share creation was halted in PGM, the ETN traded at a significant premium to its underlying value.
SOURCE: Reproduced with permission of Yahoo! Inc. © 2010 Yahoo! Inc. YAHOO! and the YAHOO! logo are registered trademarks of Yahoo! Inc.

market segments. Above all, the process of share creation, redemption, and intraday trading is designed to keep exchange-traded products in line with their underlying indexes. The presence of market makers and the opportunity for arbitrage help funds track their NAVs closely (shown as IVs in Figure 7.5). That's what makes PGM particularly problematic. The fund's average daily trading volume had been nearly 100,000 shares, which showed that were are plenty of buyers and sellers. However, the fund has traded at large premiums and discounts to its underlying value. To illustrate the magnitude of the problem, during the three months ending March 19, 2010, PGM advanced less than 5 percent while the underlying value of its index rose more than 12 percent.

PGM's woes were due to the halt in share creation, without which the fund has been cut from its anchor, and there was no telling what kind of bubble or crash could result. (As of this writing, share creation in PGM remains suspended.) As we've said before, investors who want exposure to platinum would do well to avoid PGM and its uncertain future and consider the new physical-backed platinum ETF (PPLT).

When a futures-backed fund runs into regulatory issues, there is another out: It can close down and return investors' money. Although issuers never want to shut an ETF or an ETN, sometimes it is simply the right thing to do. Consider the trouble faced by PowerShares DB

Crude Oil Double Long ETN (DXO). In September 2009, Deutsche Bank announced it was calling the notes backing the ETN because of a "regulatory event." As you recall, "double" and "triple" funds use leverage to replicate twice or three times the movement of a particular index. In the case of DXO, the ETN offered investors the opportunity to reap twice a long exposure to crude oil.

The Financial Industry Regulatory Authority (FINRA), however, began sounding the alarm over the funds that offer double and triple exposure to the market, from the short and long side. Such leveraged exposure is not meant for investment purposes, but should only be used for intraday positions by professionals. In September 2009, FINRA came out with common-sense regulations that require double margins for two-times leveraged fund and triple margins for three-times leverage funds.

By that time, DXO had already halted share creation in response to futures restrictions from the CFTC. As a leveraged commodity fund, DXO took a double hit because both areas—leveraged funds and futures-backed funds—had been subjected to regulatory scrutiny.

There's no doubt that DXO's demise was the honorable action as it closed the fund and returned investors' money. With regulatory forces bearing down on the ETF marketplace, DXO was clearly in the crosshairs. Being futures-backed, leveraged, and in the commodity market, DXO didn't stand a chance. DXO's closure was a most unusual development for anyone in the ETF industry to watch. Normally, issuers kill off those funds that are losers: They fail to attract investors and wither on the vine, so to speak. But DXO was a popular ETN, just as United States Natural Gas (UNG) was a growing ETF. However, regulatory restrictions got the better of both of these products. In the case of UNG, it was adapt or die. For DXO, beleaguered as both futures-backed and leveraged, there was no choice but to bow out gracefully.

A footnote about what happens when a fund closes down: When a fund closes, investors received the NAV as of a specific date. If an ETF or ETN was trading at a premium due to a halt in share creation, investors do not get the benefit of that pricing bubble. After the announcement that a fund is folding up, investors can hold on until the end and receive the NAV as of the date the fund will cease trading. Or they can take their chances in the open market and try to sell. With all these unknowns, it's hard to determine what the best course of action would be. You can sell before trading is halted, but in the crush of people racing to the exit you cannot be sure that what you receive is actually what the fund is worth. If you wait until the end, your money is tied up instead of being put to use to grow your portfolio. If you are an active investor, sitting and waiting to get your money back is a big philosophical problem if nothing else.

While leveraged and futures-based DXO was done in by its popularity, it has siblings that are alive and kicking, saved by their wallflower status; among them, PowerShares DB Crude Oil Double Short ETN (DTO). The plug hasn't been pulled on DTO because it is not as popular (again, the exact opposite of what we usually see happening in ETFs). Since DTO has less investor interest, it is not yet at risk of hitting its position limits. If the oil market turns down sharply, however, DTO could see the same trouble that plagued its double-long sibling.

Commodity Exposure: A Cautionary Tale

The tale of regulatory troubles for futures-backed ETFs and ETNs brings us back to the major theme we have discussed throughout this book. What makes an exchange-traded product successful is neither its price action nor its popularity, although liquidity is certainly one of the desirable qualities of an ETF. The single most important attribute of a successful exchange-traded product is that it closely tracks its underlying value. When pricing bubbles occur because share creation has been halted, it is like any market dislocation, such as we saw a few years ago in housing and a decade ago in technology stocks. When there is a disconnect between what people are buying and selling and what something is really worth, there is bound to be trouble. We have witnessed the aftermath of bubbles on a smaller scale in futures-backed products such as UNG, PGM, and DXO. Given the dislocations that have occurred with futures-based ETFs, investors must consider themselves forewarned.

In the ideal world, ETF issuers would be able to offer the exposure that investors want without an overhanging regulatory threat. The funds would closely track their NAVs, and all parties would get what they want: The investor has access to a desired market through a transparent strategy; a fund issuer enjoys the success of an exchange-traded product that attracts assets; and market makers and authorized participants have strong order flow. With commodity ETFs the story is not so simple.

With equity-based ETFs the objective is to gain exposure to a specific sector or index, while mitigating the risk posed by a single stock. If there are 100 stocks in an equity index and one runs into trouble, the impact will most likely be minimal. Even if the stock is among the larger holdings in the index, the fallout will be muted by other companies in the index.

With futures-based commodity funds, however, there are more risks not only because of the nature of the derivative markets, but because of regulatory limitations that could affect ETFs and ETNs that hold futures contracts. The futures-based fund you bought yesterday may suddenly disconnect from its basis because share creation has been halted, or the fund may have to substitute swaps for futures in its portfolio.

Even without what some might see as external interference, there are other issues with a fund based upon futures, swaps, or a combination of both. Your exposure to the desired market is being replicated by a particular instrument. You have not "gone to the source," as it were; you are still a step or two away. You're not buying gold—you are buying gold futures; the same applies with natural gas or crude oil.

The further away you are from your desired market, the less transparent things become. If you want to be involved in commodities, try to get as close to the real thing as possible. Physically backed funds in gold, silver, platinum, and palladium are as real as you can get without holding the metal in your hands. You own a piece of a stockpile, the price of which will rise or fall based upon forces of supply and demand in the market for the physical material. Of course, such exposure is not possible with all commodities.

Therefore, you need to consider the next best thing: the commodity producers. Equity-based alternatives can still give you exposure to

the commodity—whether gold, natural gas, oil, or another substance—
through the companies that produce, process, and transport them.
Even though it's not the same as a physically backed fund, the equity
alternative restores transparency and takes away the possibility of regulatory limits that could affect trading.

As the ETF industry endures its adolescent stage, ongoing regulatory reform will prevent some funds from achieving their primary
objectives: that is, efficiently tracking their underlying net asset value.
As you pursue your investment objectives, you must look beyond the
name of a fund to determine the best approach to meet your needs.
It is up to you to make sure you know what you are getting and
keep abreast with developments that could impact your portfolio.

Chapter 8

Staying Current with TIPS and Currencies

Since the first domestic equity ETF was launched, product choices have increased dramatically to include international, commodity, leveraged, and actively managed funds, and everything in between. Wherever and whenever there is investor interest in products that provide exposure to certain market segments or sectors, there will be ETFs to meet that demand. In this chapter, we look at two types of ETFs with specific and timely objectives in mind: inflation protection and currency exposure. Traditionally, these investment themes have been off the radar for most people because of the complexity of executing these strategies. Now, thanks to ETFs, gaining exposure to currencies or protecting one's portfolio from the threat of inflation in the future is as easy as buying shares in a tradable vehicle.

In order to make your investment decisions, you need to be watchful of market conditions as well as economic and geopolitical developments. Inflation or currency investments require a global view.

Dealing with Inflation

Inflation has been on many investors' minds, given the massive stimulus program rolled out by the U.S. government. As of this writing in the first quarter of 2010, inflation fears have not sparked any tangible flames of concern. However, given the passage of a $940 billion health care bill, one has to wonder what the impact of all this spending will be on the United States' already considerable financial burden. Forecasts clearly show that the budget deficit will widen and debt levels will get higher.

Thus far, inflation has not been a problem. Investors, however, might be inclined to add the word "yet." Many economists and market strategists have also concluded that the U.S. economy will likely face heightened expectations for inflation, especially in the long term.

Inflation worries are particularly acute for one particular investment demographic: aging baby boomers who are increasingly concerned about getting by on a fixed income. If inflation heats up, what will the impact be on their portfolios—and their retirement lifestyles? Fortunately, investors do not have to sit back and wring their hands, feeling powerless. Although they certainly can't control inflation, they can respond to this potential threat with ETFs that track Treasury Inflation-Protected Securities, known as TIPS.

Demand for TIPS ETFs has been rising. To illustrate, in the fall of 2009, two of the biggest net-asset gainers among all ETFs were SPDR Gold (GLD), which, as discussed in Chapter 7, tracks a physical stockpile of gold, and iShares Barclays TIPS Bond Fund (TIP). Although there may have been many reasons why investors were adding GLD to their portfolios, the appeal of a fund such as TIP is clearly related to inflation fears. In fact, the money that investors poured into TIP in late 2009 was a strong indication of widespread desire to build inflation protection into portfolios.

Given the increasing popularity of TIPS ETFs, let's take a closer look at these products so you can gain a better understanding of how these securities work, and what offerings provide the exposure that you may be seeking. TIPS are bonds whose principal is linked to the Consumer Price Index (CPI). When the CPI increases, the principal in the TIPS bonds is adjusted upward. As a result, TIPS coupons are paid on a higher principal.

During times of deflation, however, the TIPS principal is adjusted downward. If you owned a TIPS fund during a deflationary period, the distribution would be suspended. Therefore, while owning a TIPS ETF would help protect you during times of inflation, you could not count on it to provide regular income during deflationary times.

As we've seen across the ETF industry, issuers are increasing their offerings of focused products. Rather than stick with a broad category or sector, funds are slicing and dicing markets to offer funds that have a narrower focus; for example, offering a specific commodity and not just a broad commodity index, or focusing on a single country instead of a geographic region. This same phenomenon is present in TIPS, as issuers look for ways to capitalize on investor interest in protecting their portfolios from the possibility of higher inflation in the future. The variation in TIPS ETFs has to do with maturities of the securities, from short-term to long-term.

TIPS are issued with different maturities, just like bonds. The longer the time to maturity, the more volatility the fund will experience. Therefore, while longer-term TIPS investments such as the PIMCO 15+ Year TIPS ETF (LTPZ) may be more beneficial for investors with longer-term time frames, buying this fund would expose you to more volatility than you would experience with an ETF that tracks TIPS with shorter maturities.

When you select a TIPS fund, consider the expectations for changes in real yields over time. Real yields rise due to economic growth and hikes in short-term interest rates. If you expect real yields to increase in the short term, you would most likely favor TIPS ETFs with shorter maturities and shorter durations. If you expect real rates to fall in the short term, you would favor TIPS ETFs with longer underlying maturities and longer durations.

Keep in mind that these instruments work best in a "stagflationary" environment, marked by low economic growth and high or rising inflation. During these periods, TIPS funds have the potential to outperform Treasuries and equities. Using funds that allow you to target your time frame might be especially appealing. TIPS ETFs are also beneficial as part of a buy-and-hold strategy. While it is true that a period of rising inflation may provide even more reason to add TIPS to your portfolio, these funds can be complementary to the fixed-income portion of your investments, and may be beneficial over the long term to diversify your bond holdings. Thus, even as an active investor, you may want to consider TIPS funds when you think there is a greater likelihood of worsening inflation over the next few years. After all, there is only one direction for interest rates to move; eventually they will go up. No matter how much people talk about a low-interest rate environment now and in the near term, eventually rates will rise. Therefore, investors should consider using TIPS ETFs to build in long-term portfolio protection.

Here are some offerings to consider. iShares Barclays TIPS Bond Fund (TIP) enjoys first-mover status in the TIPS ETF category. TIP is a liquid, well-constructed ETF with a low expense ratio. TIP uses a laddered structure to create an underlying index that contains securities with a range of maturities, as illustrated in Table 8.1. As you can see, the largest percentage holding as of March 2010 was of securities that mature in 1 to 5 years, followed by those with a 5- to 10-year maturity time frame. Average maturity was 9.07 years.

Owning TIP may not deliver the same rush as trading in and out of sector ETFs, but over the long term it could be very satisfying. TIP also serves as a reminder of how ETFs can play a larger role in long-term money management.

As we have seen elsewhere in ETFs, when one issuer opens the door, others try to rush in. Although iShares was the first with TIP,

Table 8.1 Range of maturities of securities held in iShares Barclays TIPS (TIP)

0–1 years	0.00%
1–5 years	37.74%
5–10 years	31.27%
10–15 years	5.63%
15–20 years	22.01%
20–25 years	1.36%
25 years and over	1.49%
Average	9.07 years

Note: Maturity as of 3/18/2010
SOURCE: iShares.

which was introduced in December 2003, other funds have since followed. One such offering is SPDR Barclays Capital TIPS (IPE), which was launched in May 2007. Its modified adjusted duration, as of March 19, 2010, was 8.05 years, and its real adjusted duration was 7.79 years. Although IPE has a slightly lower management fee than TIP, it has yet to attract strong investor interest.

PIMCO, meanwhile, launched three products in 2009 to compete with TIP and IPE. PIMCO Broad TIPS (TIPZ) is an intermediate duration fund with an effective maturity (as of February 2010) of 9.01 years. PIMCO 1–5 Year TIPS (STPZ), as the name implies, has a shorter-term focus, investing in securities with a remaining term to final maturity of at least one year and less than five years. As of February 2010, its effective maturity was 3.17 years. PIMCO 15+ Year TIPS (LTPZ) targets long-term TIPS. As of March 2010, its effective duration was 11.71 years.

Given PIMCO's expertise in fixed income, it makes perfect sense that this issuer would launch three TIPS products. As inflation protection becomes more popular with investors, you can expect more issuers will also capitalize on the trend with funds of their own. As an investor, you must consider what a competing fund has to offer. Expense ratio? A particular expertise? As you pick and choose among TIPS ETFs, keep a careful eye on objective, strategy and, of course, the liquidity of the fund. Remember, just because something is new (particularly in the ETF world), that doesn't make it better. You have to think about what a particular product adds to the marketplace, and what value or edge the issuer is offering.

Not all TIPS ETFs are created equal, and not all of the new funds will measure up to the standards of their forebears. Once again, this highlights the importance of suitability for you—and not just in the TIPS category, but across the spectrum of investment choices. TIPS ETFs are worth exploring, but take care to choose the most appropriate fund.

Currencies

The currency market is a perfect example of a sector that typically was off-limits to retail investors. In the past, even if you were aware of the dollar rising or falling or you had an opinion about a foreign currency like the British pound or the Canadian dollar, it was not very likely that you would start trading currencies. With ETFs today, however, you can gain the currency exposure you desire. This is very similar to what we are seeing with commodities: using ETFs to gain access to part of the market that may now be attractive to the average investor. Currency ETFs are yet another example of the adaptability of this instrument to various markets.

The most basic offerings are ETFs that track a single currency. CurrencyShares, for example, offers an extensive list of single-currency ETFs that aim to replicate the investment benefits of holding foreign currency. Its single-currency products provide access to the Australian dollar, British pound, Canadian dollar, Euro, Japanese yen, Mexican peso, Russian ruble, Swedish krona, and Swiss franc.

To illustrate the appeal of these products, let's take a look at a single-currency fund and the kind of market conditions that might prompt an active investor like you to seek a particular exposure. In early 2010, the Canadian dollar was continuing to strengthen, thanks to a growing economy in Canada, a stabilizing unemployment rate, and a trade surplus. One negative factor was a decline in crude oil prices, which was affecting the Canadian dollar, given the country's role as a large exporter of total petroleum products, particularly to the United States. Overall, the favorable outlook in Canada was prompting many investors to "go loonie"—that is, to seek exposure to the Canadian dollar, which is nicknamed the "loonie" after the common loon depicted on the back of the dollar coin. One way to accomplish that exposure was through CurrencyShares Canadian Dollar Trust (FXC), as shown in Figure 8.1.

If you're interested in trading currency ETFs, most likely your positions will be relatively short-term. The reason is that currencies may not trend in a particular direction over time. However, ETFs offer a fairly easy way to seek exposure to currencies in order to capitalize on an economic development or other situation. For example, in early 2010 the debt crisis in Greece created a great deal of economic uncertainty in Europe that hit the euro. As Greece sought a financial bailout, many investors were seeking to be short the euro.

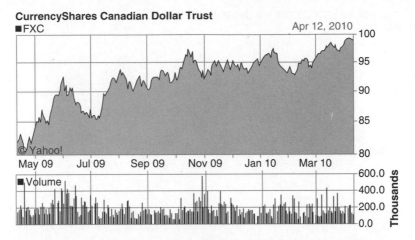

Figure 8.1 One-year chart for CurrencyShares Canadian Dollar
Trust (FXC) reflects a strengthening Canadian dollar.
SOURCE: Reproduced with permission of Yahoo! Inc. © 2010 Yahoo! Inc. YAHOO!
and the YAHOO! logo are registered trademarks of Yahoo! Inc.

Aggressive daily traders could use the ProShares UltraShort Euro
ETF (EUO) for short-term trades. An important word of caution
here: EUO seeks *daily* investment results, before fees and expenses,
which are twice the opposite performance of the U.S. dollar price of
the euro. This leveraged, inverse fund is for very short-term positions
and should be used only by aggressive daily traders who watch the
market full-time.

Long-term investors could still seek exposure, but with a different ETF: the PowerShares DB US Dollar Index Bullish ETF (UUP).
This fund seeks to replicate the performance of being long the U.S.
dollar against a basket of currencies including the euro, Japanese yen,
British pound, Canadian dollar, Swedish krona, and Swiss franc. If
you expect European currencies to weaken, then UUP would be a
consideration for your portfolio (see Figure 8.2). Should you hold the
opposite view and expect the U.S. dollar to decline against foreign
currencies, a fund to consider is PowerShares DB US Dollar Bearish
Fund (UDN), which seeks to replicate the performance of being short
the U.S. dollar against the euro, yen, pound, Canadian dollar, krona,
and Swiss franc.

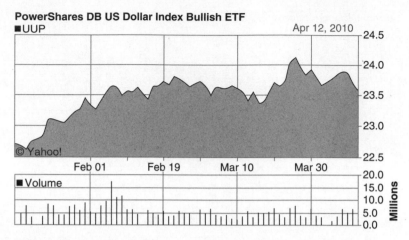

Figure 8.2 Three-month chart for PowerShares DB U.S. Dollar Index Bullish ETF (UUP) shows the overall gain in the dollar versus other currencies.

SOURCE: Reproduced with permission of Yahoo! Inc. © 2010 Yahoo! Inc. YAHOO! and the YAHOO! logo are registered trademarks of Yahoo! Inc.

Other single-currency offerings include funds such as the WisdomTree Dreyfus Chinese Yuan Fund (CYB), which seeks to achieve total returns reflective of both money market rates in China available to foreign investors and changes in the value of the Chinese yuan relative to the U.S. dollar. Given the long-term growth potential in China, many investors have been flocking to CYB.

WisdomTree also offers exposure to other single currencies through funds such as its Brazilian Real Fund (BZF), Indian Rupee Fund (ICN), and South African Rand Fund (SZR). Because of government restrictions and capital controls, as well as liquidity in some cases, WisdomTree funds use forward contracts, known as nondeliverable forwards, to replicate currency exposure. A forward contract is an agreement to exchange currencies for a given rate at a specific date; in other words, the price at which one currency will be exchanged for another. The benefit of these contracts is that they allow a foreign investor to approximate the return of a money market fund denominated in a different currency. In some cases, the return is very close to the actual rate of interest in a country.

In addition to holding a single currency, there are also ETFs that offer exposure to baskets of multiple currencies. For example, the WisdomTree Dreyfus Emerging Currency Fund (CEW) seeks to achieve returns that reflect money market rates in select emerging markets available to foreign investors and changes in the value of these currencies versus the U.S. dollar. CEW targets several currencies including the Mexican peso, Brazilian real, Chilean peso, South African rand, Polish zloty, Israeli shekel, Turkish new lira, Chinese yuan, South Korean won, Taiwanese dollar, and Indian rupee.

As we've seen time and again in various sectors of the market, not all ETFs are alike. Just as a commodity ETF that tracks the physical metal is far different (and less prone to risk) than those that hold futures, the same lesson applies in currencies. A single currency fund that tracks a major currency such as the euro or British pound is not the same as an ETF that invests in several currencies using futures contracts.

Consider the PowerShares DB G10 Currency Harvest Fund (DBV), which tracks an index composed of currency futures contracts on certain G10 currencies, as mentioned in Chapter 3. DBV target currencies include the U.S. dollar, euro, Japanese yen, Canadian dollar, Swiss franc, British pound, Australian dollar, New Zealand dollar, Norwegian krone, and Swedish krona.

No matter how appealing this may sound, investor beware! DBV recently earned the number four spot on our 10 Most Dangerous ETFs for buy and hold investors, and for good reason. As we see it, going for incremental returns while taking on huge potential risk is like picking up pennies in front of a steamroller. The reason? DBV's strategy is based on the "carry trade," which is one of the oldest of all trading strategies. The carry trade involves borrowing in a currency with low interest rates and investing the money in another currency with higher rates. Specifically, DBV borrows the three lowest-yielding currencies and invests in the three highest yielding.

The goal is to make small profits over time. Historically, higher-yielding currencies maintain their exchange rate against lower-yielding currencies or even appreciate slightly. This allows traders to lock in the difference between the two yields. DBV, however, uses leverage to increase the profits that otherwise would probably be rather small. The problem is that this strategy tends to fall apart during times of economic turmoil or if the tide shifts in the currency markets. When the trend reverses, a carry trade can lose its gains very quickly.

PowerShares acknowledges the risks, noting that currencies and futures in general are volatile and not suitable for all investors. It also cites the risk of investing in foreign exchange-related products that are subject to many factors that can increase volatility, including national debt levels and trade deficits, changes in domestic and foreign interest rates, and expectations regarding interest rates, currency exchange rates, and global or regional economic or financial events. Don't consider this the perfunctory boilerplate. DBV is a speculative fund that uses leverage in currency markets, which can be very volatile. If you want exposure to currency, there are safer ETFs.

Summing It Up

As we have discussed, each sector of the ETF market has its peculiarities. The products we've focused on in this chapter, TIPS and currency ETFs, have their unique qualities as well. TIPS are often used for long-term portfolio protection and money management to fend off the effects of inflation, which is expected to worsen in the future. Although no one knows when inflation will become a problem, it seems virtually certain that at some point in the future it will be an issue.

ETFs that offer exposure to currencies are meant for shorter-term directional trades to gain exposure to, for example, the U.S. dollar or a foreign currency. Keep in mind that currencies are not like buying a technology fund or a financial sector ETF. No matter how narrowly focused an equity sector fund is, it will be composed of several securities. A currency ETF that focuses on, say, the euro tracks just that one thing. As you look to make a profit from a currency move or to hedge exposure to an international investment elsewhere in your portfolio, the currency ETFs that you will use are very narrowly defined and not well diversified. In addition, buying a currency ETF should not be confused with buying an ETF that focuses on a particular market through equity exposure. In other words, buying a Brazilian real ETF is not the same as owning shares of an international equity ETF that invests in companies in Brazil.

One of the good things about a currency ETF is that the underlying markets are huge. Unlike, say, platinum futures that are thinly traded, currency markets are highly liquid and dominated by institutional players. You never have to worry that a currency ETF will suddenly become too large for the market it tracks. Therefore, the last thing you want to do is shoot yourself in the foot by using an illiquid ETF in order to gain access to such a liquid market. We've said it before, but it bears repeating: Look at the fund volume, and not just for one day but a three-month average. Is there sufficient volume to keep pricing fair and in line with the NAV?

There are simply too many choices to settle for an illiquid, thinly traded ETF. As an investor, you are in the proverbial driver's seat. The fund issuers want and need you—not the other way around. Do your homework, research your options, and always choose what's right for you, your portfolio, your investment time horizon, and your risk tolerance. Whatever your objective, chances are there are plenty of ETF choices to consider—and even more on the way.

Part III

TYING IT
ALL TOGETHER

Chapter 9

Looking Ahead: A Changed Landscape

Pressured by the tectonic forces of competition and regulation, the ETF landscape continues to shift and change. What lies ahead is new and unfamiliar terrain. We're all in this together, both industry experts and those who are new to these funds. Using what we've learned thus far, we move forward into uncharted territory that is marked with a new level of complexity. Although there are unknowns, we look to the features that have distinguished ETFs in the past—transparency, liquidity, and low costs—to guide us on our journey ahead.

Based on the latest developments, funds that use derivatives, swaps, and futures contracts could see the biggest changes, thanks to greater scrutiny and additional regulation that appears almost certain as of this writing. By the end of the first quarter of 2010, regulatory authorities were making good on what had been promised (or threatened, depending upon how you look at it) for the past year: more oversight for funds that use derivatives, the risks of which retail investors may not adequately understand.

For the fund industry, it is a double-barreled challenge coming from both the Securities and Exchange Commission (SEC) and the Commodity Futures Trading Commission (CFTC). Both regulatory bodies have set their sights on exchange-traded products in a way that has set a new tone for regulatory changes, which will impact the types of funds that will be introduced in the future. Wisely, actions by the SEC and CFTC have not impacted funds that are already launched and trading. However, the two agencies have targeted the pipeline of proposed offerings, which will really get the fund industry's attention.

As of this writing, the outcome of the SEC and CFTC regulatory reviews is not known. However, there is little question that additional regulatory scrutiny can be expected in the future. In addition, funds may be subjected to new rules and requirements on such things as the size and types of derivative holdings, how they implement risk management, and how risks involved with derivatives are communicated to investors in prospectus materials.

The SEC announced its regulatory review in late March 2010, focusing on actively managed and leveraged ETFs that rely on swaps and other derivative instruments to achieve their investment objectives. As regulators had pointed out even before the SEC announcement was made, sophisticated short-term strategies employed by derivative-based leveraged ETFs and derivative-based commodity ETFs and ETNs can pose a significant risk to investors who do not understand the fund objectives. As a result of the SEC action, several firms that had filed for new actively managed funds had their requests put on hold. The rush to launch actively managed funds, which garner much higher fees than their more traditional ETF brethren, came to a standstill, at least for the moment.

Meanwhile, the CFTC was mulling its own plan to impose stricter position limits on ETFs and ETNs that are backed by futures contracts. Of particular concern were funds that track commodities of finite supply. The CFTC has wanted to ensure that funds do not become so big that their futures contract positions end up distorting the markets that they are supposed to track. As you recall from Chapter 7, one fund that has raised concern among regulators is iPath Dow Jones-UBS Platinum Subindex Total Return^{SM} ETN (PGM), which is based on platinum futures—a very thinly traded market.

When PGM grew because of investor interest in gaining exposure to platinum, the CFTC became wary, and the fund was subjected to new futures safety limits.

CFTC action has also targeted energy ETFs, such as those that offer exposure to crude oil and natural gas futures, as well as other derivative-backed funds that track metals such as gold and nickel. As of this writing, the CFTC had not taken action to investigate funds that track soft commodities such as cocoa and sugar, although it may be only a matter of time before funds that trade these futures are included in the discussion.

If the CFTC succeeds in making position limits for derivative-based ETFs more widespread, this could potentially limit the size of the funds that trade these markets. Position limits cap the number of future contracts that any single fund can carry. If funds cannot gain access to more futures, they cannot create additional shares, which stifles the growth of the fund—and results in a premium when there is more demand than shares available.

Although the SEC and CFTC have taken two different approaches to ETF regulation, both agencies share a common focus: funds that use derivatives to achieve their objectives. Some ETFs that are overseen by both agencies could be particularly vulnerable. For example, PowerShares DB Gold Double Long ETN (DGP) not only tracks a finite commodity, it also uses leverage. A fund of this type could be in for significant regulatory review.

In a statement, SEC Chairman Mary Schapiro called a more thorough review of the use of derivatives by ETFs and other instruments "appropriate." Andrew Donohue, director of the SEC's Division of Investment Management, added that the use of derivatives by funds was not new. However, the agency wanted "to be sure our regulatory protections keep up with the increasing complexity of these instruments and how they are used by fund managers. This is the right time to take a step back and rethink those protections."[1]

[1]SEC.gov, "SEC Staff Evaluating the Use of Derivatives by Funds," Securities and Exchange Commission Press Release, March 25, 2010 http://www.sec.gov/news/press/2010/2010-45.htm.

The right time, indeed. Exchange-traded products have gone increasingly mainstream with more exposure in money management accounts and even 401(k) accounts. The industry is salivating over the multi-trillion-dollar retirement market, which has been the bailiwick of mutual funds. It seems logical that, before ETFs make greater headway into the retail market, regulators would engage in further review and perhaps introduce additional regulation regarding investor education and protection.

Actions by the regulators should not have come as any surprise, given the political and regulatory environment. By early 2010, the Administration was celebrating a victory over health care reform and moving forward with attempts to rein in the financial industry. Would it be any surprise, then, that regulators would look at how exchange-traded products, which have experienced explosive growth, are using derivatives to execute strategies aimed at the average retail investor?

The ETF industry has been going through its growing pains, which we've described as an awkward, adolescent phase. Just as every teenager needs rules (although wanting them is an entirely different matter), the ETF industry is probably due for some stricter guidelines. Given the growth that ETFs have experienced, especially over the past decade, increased regulatory oversight seems like a given. It's doubtful that even more stringent rules for leveraged and derivative-based products will hurt the potential of this industry, which continues to experience strong inflows of investor assets.

It should not be up to the regulators, alone, to determine how ETFs are launched and managed. As we'll discuss in more depth in this chapter, the ETF industry could do a better job of self-policing to stave off further regulatory intervention, without killing off innovation that has been the lifeblood of the ETF industry. Interesting, that was the point made by the Financial Industry Regulatory Authority (FINRA).

FINRA has certainly been vocal in the past about the need to educate investors and protect them from inappropriate, high-risk leveraged products. For example, in June 2009, FINRA warned brokers about selling leveraged ETFs that offer double and triple market exposure to retail investors. A few months later, FINRA sent out a special alert about increased margin requirements for leveraged ETFs, targeting the "ultra-long" and "ultra-short" strategies.

At the time of the SEC and CFTC reviews, however, FINRA Chairman Richard Ketchum said he did not favor restricting the creation of new securities products. "I'm not a big fan of prohibiting product innovation," Ketchum said at the time. "But we are looking at the product pipeline, how it's controlled and managed by the firms, and we'll see whether other regulation is necessary."

Nonetheless, FINRA, which has issued both warnings to the industry and fines to specific firms regarding the sale of complex products without adequate investor education, continues to worry about suitability. To that end, Ketchum said FINRA has been working to understand the development of new products, which have undergone explosive growth over the past 10 years, touching off regulatory concern. "One thing we're looking hard at is how do we make sure we get a handle and see up front the stuff that is coming through the pipeline. That's really where our focus is. This is a huge concern for us."[2]

With the SEC, CFTC, and FINRA watching, the ETF industry needs to take action on its own, not only with boilerplate disclaimers, but with better investor education. Admittedly, the ETF industry has done a better job of informing investors about the unsuitability of certain products, especially leveraged funds whose purpose is to gain exposure for a day—not the longer term. But more needs to be done.

As for you, the investor, regulatory reviews are ultimately for your own good. As you've seen, the ETF industry has bombarded the marketplace with new offerings. Issuers have sometimes launched funds by the half-dozen at one time. Among exchange-traded products, "new" has often become a synonym for "more complex." Therefore, regulatory intervention, if nothing else, had made the industry stop and consider what's being offered to the investing public. Such a pause at this time seems prudent.

[2]Herbert Lash, "FINRA eyes new rules for ETF products," Reuters.com, March 29, 2010, http://www.reuters.com/article/idUSTRE62S4H520100329.

The regulatory crackdown on ETFs should prompt you to become more cautious when managing your investment portfolio. Although the agencies' focus is on new products in the pipeline, their worries about whether investors understand what they're getting should also be your personal concern. Unless you are a sophisticated investor, should you really be using leverage or commodity futures–backed ETFs and ETNs to achieve a specific goal? Chances are you should avoid these types of funds at least until the regulatory uncertainty passes. Remember, the ETFs that serve you best are those that adhere to the three basic principles of a good fund: transparency, liquidity, and low cost.

Investors, it seems, have been paying attention. The first quarter of 2010 marked the comeback of the iconic fund: the tried-and-true products such as SPDR S&P 500 ETF (SPY), which in February 2010 was the biggest gainer of fund flows. The first U.S.-listed ETF ever and the largest, SPY gained more than $1.5 billion in investor monies in February. This came after a huge drop in assets the month before, which had made it the biggest loser in January 2010. PowerShares QQQ (QQQQ), which had also lost considerable assets in January, powered back in February to be the third-largest asset gainer in that month with inflows of $872 million.

Despite the appeal of these enduring classics, however, the fund industry has been more enamored with the new, the complex, and the not-so-transparent, which net a higher fee. With more actively managed funds being pushed into the market in hopes of attracting retail investors, it's no wonder that regulators stepped in when they did.

Victims of Their Own Success

You have to hand it to the ETF industry: They know how to make money. At first, there were the copycat funds. Issuers such as Vanguard and Schwab helped to push down fund fees with lookalike products that were cheaper than offerings from the first movers. By charging less for funds, issuers hope to attract volume from investors. But that's not the only way to make money in this industry.

ETF issuers are also looking to charge higher fees for more exotic products: complex leveraged, commodity, and actively managed funds. Looking at announcements of new funds that have been launched in the first quarter of 2010, prior to the regulatory review, it was apparent that most of the products were derivative-based. For example, the first NYSE-listed ETF of 2010 was the WisdomTree International Hedged Equity Fund (HEDJ), which uses derivatives to hedge equity exposure. New funds were not coming out one at a time, either. In early 2010, ProShares launched 11 new leveraged products on the NYSE—with 6 of them introduced on the same day in February.

Investors may not understand how complex derivative-based products work, but the issuers sure know how to get paid for them. For example, ProShares' UltraPro Russell 2000 (URTY), UltraPro QQQ (TQQQ), UltraPro Mid-Cap 400 (UMDD), and UltraPro Dow 30 (UDOW), launched in February 2010, have expense ratios of 0.95 percent. By contrast, the iShares S&P 500 Index Fund (IVV) has an expense ratio of only 0.09 percent.

Of course, fund issuers and many investors would argue that the new, sophisticated products have provided access to markets and complex strategies that previously were off-limits to many investors. As they see it, there is value in giving investors more choice with a wide array of products offering exposure to everything from domestic equity indexes to exotic futures markets. Granted, when it comes to ingenuity and providing open access to the market, ETF issuers have certainly proven their abilities. At the same time, we have to wonder if it's really appropriate for investors to be uniformly granted access to complex strategies in the first place. Perhaps the way to attack the problem is to require ETF investors to meet certain requirements, as is done in options trading, before they can trade complex, derivative-based instruments.

Exotic ETFs should be isolated in a different category away from other ETF products. That way, a clearer distinction could be drawn between traditional and nontraditional ETFs; each with a different set of disclosure requirements and even marketing materials. It's easy to envision that these products would be separated even at the web site level so that, as an average retail investor, you would not even be able to see funds that were inappropriate for you. Only those who declare themselves to be sophisticated investors would be able to access information on leveraged and derivative-based funds. Once you crossed through the warnings and disclaimers, you would know for certain that the sophisticated—and more expensive—products are not the same as the traditional ETFs.

In time we will gain a fuller understanding of the consequences of the regulatory review, as well as what the industry itself might do to more proactively police itself. At the same time, the industry might want to think about how it can better protect investors by providing more education. Going for fees and money flow alone is shortsighted and potentially endangers all involved. When it comes to the issuers, it could be a case of biting the hand that feeds them. A better alternative would be to realign ETF issuer interests with those of the investors. In other words, it's time to look at the motivation.

In their defense, ETF issuers probably had no way of predicting just how successful certain products would be, or that their funds would grow so large that they could actually dominate the markets they were trying to track, as in the case of United States Natural Gas (UNG), which suddenly faced natural gas futures contract position limits that stunted its growth. Who could have seen that as ETFs offered access to markets that had been very limited, everyday investors would jump on the bandwagon for exposure to such things as natural gas and platinum futures? Some of it may be good marketing. United States Natural Gas does sound like the General Motors of commodities, with all the assurance of USDA prime beef. Despite the homegrown name, UNG is really an exotic fund. Therein lies the real issue. ETF issuers need to think about what they are branding before they put their stamp on it.

Let's take a step back and remind ourselves how the ETF game is played. For the fund issuer, it's all about devising new ideas in hopes of attracting investor interest, which translates into assets flowing into the fund. For the market makers, investor interest means order flow, allowing them to make more money even with a narrow spread between the bid and the ask. As for you, the investor, you want a variety of products that will enable you to execute your particular strategy, whether as an active trader looking to target certain sectors for the short term or with a longer-term base of exposure to the broad indexes.

The problem, however, is that the number of funds that actually meets the needs of all parties—issuers, market makers, and investors—is far less than the number that is launched. Fund issuers know that out of, say, six new funds, only one really has to make it in order to pay for the rest. The other five can limp along with low liquidity, and one could even be folded up in the future. In other words, launching ETFs has become a numbers game, as we have seen with a proliferation of new products over the past year or so. Does the investing public really need double or triple leveraged exposure to a certain industry sector? Is there really enough interest in investing in an obscure emerging market?

Consider a filing made on March 5, 2010, by Eaton Vance to launch five actively managed funds—the Eaton Vance Enhanced Short Maturity ETF, Government Limited Maturity ETF, Intermediate Municipal Bond ETF, Prime Limited Maturity ETF, and Short Term Municipal Bond ETF. Does the issuer really believe that all five of these actively managed funds would make it? Success, after all, does not come when a fund is finally approved and launched. The measure of a successful ETF, as we have said all along, is closely tracking its underlying value. Funds that truly offer unique advantages for investors—while adhering to the principles of transparency, liquidity, and low cost—are those that will attract assets over the long term.

Actively managed ETFs, despite their popularity among issuers, have actually underperformed as a category. Sure, ETF issuers can charge more for them, but not a single one could hold a candle to, say, the SPDR S&P (SPY) or the PowerShares QQQ (QQQQ). The fact is, actively managed ETFs have failed to draw investor interest because they lack the fundamental attributes of a good ETF—once again, transparency, liquidity, and low cost. What will it take for issuers to get it?

Instead of the "try it, you'll like it" school of launching ETFs to investors, what if the issuers themselves had some skin in the game? This brings to mind the January 2008 launch of the Greenhaven Continuous Community Index Fund (GCC), designed to deliver broad-based diversified commodity exposure. GCC's launch was notable because it was brought to market through a partnership between the issuer and the specialist firm. Both parties were aligned in the success of the product.

As the ETF industry moves forward and matures, more alignment is needed that will encourage issuers to be more responsible about the funds they create. Issuers, in particular, need to align their interests more closely with those of investors. Consider what happens with an initial public offering (IPO). When a privately held company goes public, the founders usually still hold significant stakes. The attitude is not "sell the shares and see what happens." The principals of the firm are still shareholders; it's in their best interest to position the company to attract investor interest and produce a sustainable return on investment. Something similar could be applied to ETFs so that issuers, too, would end up holding enough shares of the funds they create to make a difference in their motivation. Issuers would be more discerning in what they launch because they are motivated to have a bigger success rate than, say, one or two in six.

It remains to be seen whether something like this will materialize in the ETF industry. Nonetheless, it's time for all parties involved to consider what steps can be taken to ensure the growth of the industry without outside forces hampering its creativity.

Searching for Opportunity

Issuers have not exactly waited patiently for the SEC and CFTC to conclude their regulatory reviews. Instead, they have sought ways to keep their pipelines flowing. Direxion, which is known for leveraged funds such as its Direxion Daily Financial Bull 3X ETF (FAS) and Direxion Daily Financial Bear 3X ETF (FAZ), listed six of its existing ETFs in Europe on the NYSE Euronext Amsterdam market. It also introduced an additional two pairs that track the Russell 1000 Index and the Russell 1000 Financial Services Index. Whether or not an influx of leveraged ETFs is really what the European market needs remains to be seen. As the ETF market globalizes, and new choices— and risks—are introduced to investors, issuers should make a more concerted effort to educate retail consumers, no matter where they reside.

Taking a different tactic, PowerShares, which has a family of commodity ETN products, launched nine new domestic equity products, targeting small-cap sectors. Because they are neither leveraged nor involve futures contracts, these funds are not subject to additional regulatory scrutiny. Interestingly, the new funds target nine sectors—from consumer discretionary to utilities—all with small-cap stocks. The small-cap approach has worked well in ETFs, which seek to provide exposure to a class of stocks while avoiding security-specific risk. The PowerShares approach to use small caps to go after sectors shows how the ETF industry continues to slice and dice the markets in pursuit of a unique angle.

The PowerShares funds are all listed on NASDAQ, where designated "liquidity providers" pledged to be active in the funds during an "incubation period," described as the critical time when a fund first launches and before it is able to attract investor interest. During the time the liquidity providers are active, you wouldn't expect any tracking errors in the funds. The providers should provide sufficient liquidity to keep premiums and discounts from developing. However, once liquidity providers cease their activity, you would want to be on alert for potential tracking errors, which could conceivably arise if investor-driven liquidity is low. This is not to take away from the fact that PowerShares, in a bullish move, launched nine new equity products at once. Still, you should wait to see what happens with liquidity before taking a test drive in these funds, as in any offering in a new sector.

Looking ahead, we can expect to see more and more exchange-traded products being introduced, which shows just how robust the industry is. Unfortunately, this is happening at a time when the financial services industry has seen cutbacks. There are fewer specialist firms on the Street, and trading is becoming even more electronic, automated, and otherwise less human-intensive. ETFs will spread to a variety of exchanges—and perhaps one day, there will be an ETF-only exchange. It is easy to envision these developments in an industry that is so young and vibrant. In the midst of all this exuberance—with more and more product traffic, and fewer firms to manage the products—there is also an increased potential for accidents to happen. ETFs will continue to grow, of that we have no doubt. As that occurs, you will want to align yourself with the best of the products. To make that choice, you must educate yourself about ETF investment objectives and how the funds pursue them.

It's Time for a Change

You probably wouldn't confuse *Last Tango in Paris* and *The Sound of Music*. But even if you did, there is a system in place that would alert you to the difference between these two films. The first is rated NC-17 and the other G. The Motion Picture Association of America's rating system has done a good job of informing viewers about the appropriateness of the films. The ETF industry should pay attention. This discussion is particularly timely, given the current environment of financial industry reform. If the government is willing to take on the Wall Street powerhouses, then the ETF sector should recognize that new regulation that could inhibit the issuance or marketing of certain funds is not out of the question.

As we've seen in the past, ETF regulatory action that swoops in after the fact disrupts the markets. In Chapter 7, we discussed several examples, such as the futures-backed commodity funds that suddenly had to change their strategies or suspend share creation because of limits on their futures holdings. What's needed instead is something more proactive, coupling unbiased oversight with investor responsibility.

An effective ETF ratings system would help to classify funds without judging the suitability of their strategies. Investors would have more information to help them make good decisions for themselves (or with help from a financial professional). Investors would know that it's not enough to go by the name of the product alone. Otherwise, you could mistake *The Wizard of Oz* for *The Exorcist*—or in the case of ETFs, the G-rated SPDR S&P 500 ETF (SPY) and the R-rated Direxion Daily Large Cap Bull 3X Shares (BGU), which uses leverage to gain 300 percent daily exposure to the Russell 1000.

With an ETF rating system, investors would be forewarned before they even look more closely at the prospectus and other fund information. And as for the issuers, they could honestly say, "We warned you, but you didn't listen."

The ETF industry has grown to the point that investor education must catch up with the rate of product launches. Perhaps that will mean regulators need to step in. Or maybe the threat of regulatory intervention will prompt issuers to do this on their own. Whatever the catalyst, changes need to be made.

The industry needs to do more with investor education, and maybe spruce up the image of some of its stalwarts because, as the numbers show, ETFs that hit on all the important cylinders (transparency, liquidity, low cost) will win hands down over time. That's what was so interesting in early 2010 when the SPDR Dow Jones Industrial Average ETF Trust (DIA) got a facelift. Reintroduced to the investing public was a new, improved, and rebranded version of DIA, which had been known previously as DIAMONDS Trust, Series I. DIA started trading in 1998, swelling to $9 billion in net assets by the end of 2008. In 2009, however, DIA lost more than $1.1 billion in assets, which was after net asset inflows of $3.8 billion in 2008. With top holdings, as of this writing, of IBM (9.19 percent), 3M (6.04 percent), and Chevron (5.42 percent), DIA has enjoyed a good run. All it needed was to be spruced up a bit to remind investors that certain classics never go out of style. And as for DIA, which was up nearly 23 percent through 2009, it would be rated G—suitable for *all* investors.

Back to the Future

Remember the good old days in ETFs? It was a wide-open field of dreams where issuers could put forth their best ideas. Then the marketplace would be the judge. It was survival of the fittest, which in itself was motivation for issuers to bring their best and brightest ideas to fruition. Sometimes funds would make it; other times they would not. One fund that died on the vine was XShares' AirShares EU Carbon Allowance Fund (ASO). Admittedly not the first fund to close down and hardly the last, ASO was a narrowly focused offering and attracted very little trading volume.

And that, quite frankly, is the way it's supposed to work. Funds are launched by issuers (presumably with the best of intentions), and they either attract investors or they don't. It's a Darwinian cycle that we can see elsewhere in business, including on the grocery store shelves where sometimes a new flavor will be a hit and other times it will just fade away.

Informed investors who are guided by good education will be able to tell if a fund is suitable for them, given their risk tolerance, personalities, time frame, investment objective, and time devoted to keeping tabs on the market. Investor choice is what ultimately distinguishes between a classic and a flop. ETF issuers need to get on the bandwagon to empower investors. Otherwise, Darwin is going to be upstaged by Big Brother.

No one wants to stifle innovation, but risks must be managed. Somehow the ETF industry needs to put a system in place to educate, inform, and empower investors so they can tell when a fund is appropriate for them and when it is not. Then a derivative-based or futures-backed fund will not have to worry about attracting so much attention from the regulators because it won't be siphoning off investor funds that, quite frankly, should probably be invested in traditional products. Instead, exotic, nontraditional funds would be reserved for sophisticated investors and marketed as such. If the ETF industry can't handle the task on its own, then expect the regulators to come in with a heavy hand to make sure risks are better managed from pipeline to marketplace.

As for you, the retail investor, the choice is really yours. Given the ever-widening array of products being offered, you need to select funds that are the best for you and your portfolio. Look beyond the name alone to consider what's in the fund. As you recall, there is a world of difference between, say, iPath Dow Jones-UBS Platinum Subindex Total Return^{SM} ETN (PGM), which is based on platinum futures contracts, and ETFS Physical Platinum Shares (PPLT), which is backed by a physical stockpile of platinum. The word "platinum" is the only thing these two funds have in common. The ways they provide exposure to that market are diametrically opposed. Empower yourself with education to know the difference.

If you learn just one thing from this book, it is the importance of educating yourself. Even reading the most basic of information about the objective, the fund holdings, and the expense ratio will help you make better choices than randomly picking what sounds good. You're looking for funds that live up to the ETF standard of (once again) transparency, liquidity, and low cost. And circling back to where this discussion started at the opening of this book, think about what really makes a successful fund. That's right: It's one that closely tracks its underlying value. If a fund does not accomplish that—no matter where the price is today or is expected to be tomorrow—then why are you even considering it?

Investors are able to watch, real time, the value at which an ETF should be trading in the open marketplace. There is no question about what something is worth. ETFs are designed to answer that up front. Far too often, though, investors do not take the time to look.

An ETF's underlying value is what it is—as determined by its underlying components. The potential for arbitrage and the presence of buyers and sellers are what keep the fund in line with its underlying value. If there is no investor interest or something is wrong with the fund's pricing, investors will see gaps between market price and underlying value. Sometimes gaps are unavoidable; for example, a fund's underlying components trade in Asian markets, which are half a world and multiple time zones away. The trend that is most disconcerting, however, is the growing number of illiquid ETFs. These funds fail to capture adequate investor interest, for whatever reason. With a lack of buyer and seller interest, pricing gets skewed.

Before you purchase an ETF, be sure to check the right things: ample average daily trading volume and a good tracking record are indications that you will likely avoid an unpleasant surprise in the future. The information is there for you to find, easily and quickly. But it is up to you to look.

There are a multitude of funds for you to consider. Just keep your eyes open and your wits about you. You have the information and the confidence; you can make good choices to allow you to take advantage of one of the most exciting and revolutionary products ever to be introduced: the ETF.

APPENDIX A

ETF Ranking System

When choosing an ETF, it is important for investors to consider not only a particular fund's objectives, but also the structure and complexity of various ETF options.

This ETF ranking system is an index of all the available U.S.-listed exchange-traded funds and exchange-traded notes as of April 30, 2010. The chart includes fund name, ticker, net assets, share volume, and ranking.

The ranking system is designed to provide investors with a guide as to the complexity of a particular ETF product. While "complexity" is a somewhat subjective term, much of the material in this book deals with the various risk factors inherent in ETF/ETN products.

Here's a quick guide to the ranking system:

Rank 1: An ETF receives a ranking score of 1 if it is appropriate for the majority of ETF investors. While investors should always read a fund's prospectus before investing, these rank 1 ETFs are the least complex of U.S.-listed ETF products.

Rank 2: If an ETF receives a ranking of 2, investors should take a little extra time to research before purchasing. Most of the rank 2 ETFs are international equity funds or physically backed commodity ETFs. International, or global, ETFs should be approached with care, while physically backed commodity ETFs have some extra tax implications.

Rank 3: Most of the ETFs with rank 3 are fixed-income products designed for people who are well versed in the bond market. While many of the rank 3 products are perfectly safe for use by most investors, they warrant a ranking of 3 because they are not traditional equity-based securities. If you are interested in purchasing an ETF with a rank of 3, make sure you understand how the fund works from a structural perspective.

Rank 4: Products with a ranking of 4 require additional investment knowledge to trade them effectively. Many of the rank 4 products are leveraged ETFs/ETNs that use complex financial products to execute their underlying strategies. Also in this category are the majority of ETN products, which are subject to the credit risk of their issuers.

Rank 5: Products with a ranking of 5 have structural issues, regulatory concerns, or extremely low volume. United States Natural Gas (UNG) and United States Oil (USO), which are both being investigated by the Commodities Futures Trading Commission, appear with rankings of 5. ETFs/ETNs that have $10 million or less in assets as of April 30, 2010, also appear with rankings of 5 because low liquidity often leads to price dislocation. Investors wishing to trade an ETF/ETN with a ranking of 5 should certainly complete extra research and consider other fund alternatives.

Table A.1   Available U.S.-listed ETFs and ETNs as of April 30, 2010

ETF/ETN Name	Ticker	Net Assets	Share Volume	Ranking[1]
U.S. Equity Short				
Rydex Inverse 2× S&P Select Sector Technology	RTW	$2	0	5
Rydex Inverse 2× S&P Select Sector Health Care	RHO	$2	0	5
Rydex Inverse 2× S&P Select Sector Financial	RFN	$8	2	5
Rydex Inverse 2× S&P Select Sector Energy	REC	$2	1	5

[1] Net Assets and Share Volume in millions. Share volume reflects monthly total.

Table A.1   Continued

ETF/ETN Name	Ticker	Net Assets	Share Volume	Ranking
Rydex Inverse 2× S&P Midcap 400	RMS	$3	0	5
Rydex Inverse 2× S&P 500	RSW	$87	1	4
Rydex Inverse 2× Russell 2000	RRZ	$12	0	4
ProShares UltraShort Telecom	TLL	$2	0	5
ProShares UltraShort SmallCap 600	SDD	$17	1	4
ProShares UltraShort S&P 500	SDS	$3,195	754	4
ProShares UltraShort Russell MidCap Value	SJL	$3	0	5
ProShares UltraShort Russell MidCap Growth	SDK	$6	0	5
ProShares UltraShort Russell 3000	TWQ	$2	0	5
ProShares UltraShort Russell 2000 Value	SJH	$7	0	5
ProShares UltraShort Russell 2000 Growth	SKK	$11	0	4
ProShares UltraShort Russell 2000	TWM	$494	191	4
ProShares UltraShort Russell 1000 Value	SJF	$9	0	5
ProShares UltraShort Russell 1000 Growth	SFK	$9	0	5
ProShares UltraShort QQQ	QID	$879	314	4
ProShares UltraShort Nasdaq Biotechnology	BIS	$6	0	5
ProShares UltraShort Dow30	DXD	$498	96	4
ProShares UltraShort DJ Utilities	SDP	$6	0	5
ProShares UltraShort DJ Technology	REW	$21	3	4
ProShares UltraShort DJ Semiconductors	SSG	$23	5	4
ProShares UltraShort DJ Real Estate	SRS	$467	242	4
ProShares UltraShort DJ Oil & Gas	DUG	$181	71	4
ProShares UltraShort DJ Industrials	SIJ	$13	1	4
ProShares UltraShort DJ Health Care	RXD	$5	0	5
ProShares UltraShort DJ Financials	SKF	$581	289	4
ProShares UltraShort DJ Consumer Services	SCC	$27	1	4
ProShares UltraShort DJ Consumer Goods	SZK	$16	0	4
ProShares UltraShort DJ Basic Materials	SMN	$122	41	4
ProShares UltraPro Short S&P 500	SPXU	$218	114	4
ProShares UltraPro Short Russell 2000	SRTY	$9	3	5

(Continued)

Table A.1   Continued

ETF/ETN Name	Ticker	Net Assets	Share Volume	Ranking
ProShares UltraPro Short QQQQ	SQQQ	$13	4	4
ProShares UltraPro Short MidCap 400	SMDD	$5	0	5
ProShares UltraPro Short Dow30	SDOW	$9	1	5
ProShares Short SmallCap 600	SBB	$25	0	4
ProShares Short S&P 500	SH	$1,437	40	4
ProShares Short Russell 2000	RWM	$196	9	4
ProShares Short Real Estate	REK	$5	0	5
ProShares Short QQQ	PSQ	$174	4	4
ProShares Short Oil & Gas	DDG	$11	0	5
ProShares Short MidCap 400	MYY	$32	1	1
ProShares Short KBW Regional Bank	KRS	$6	3	5
ProShares Short Financials	SEF	$90	2	4
ProShares Short Dow30	DOG	$242	5	4
ProShares Short Basic Materials	SBM	$5	0	5
Direxion Daily Technology Bear 3×	TYP	$58	18	4
Direxion Daily SmallCap Bear 3×	TZA	$507	619	4
Direxion Daily Real Estate Bear 3×	DRV	$76	101	4
Direxion Daily MidCap Bear 3×	MWN	$12	2	4
Direxion Daily LargeCap Bear 3×	BGZ	$257	116	4
Direxion Daily Financials Bear 3×	FAZ	$1,062	1,667	4
Direxion Daily Energy Bear 3×	ERY	$73	54	4
Barclays Short D Leveraged S&P 500 ETN	BXDD	$2	0	5
Barclays Short C Leveraged S&P 500 ETN	BXDC	$4	0	5
Barclays Short B Leveraged S&P 500 ETN	BXDB	$4	0	5
U.S. Equity Long				
WisdomTree Total Earnings	EXT	$48	0	1
WisdomTree Total Dividend	DTD	$135	0	1
WisdomTree Small Cap Earnings	EES	$107	0	1
WisdomTree Small Cap Dividend	DES	$192	1	1
WisdomTree Mid Cap Earnings	EZM	$71	0	1
WisdomTree Mid Cap Dividend	DON	$139	1	1
WisdomTree Large Cap Value	EZY	$36	0	1
WisdomTree Large Cap Growth	ROI	$16	0	1
WisdomTree Large Cap Dividend	DLN	$412	1	1
WisdomTree Earnings 500	EPS	$82	0	1
WisdomTree Dividend ex-Financials	DTN	$200	1	1
Vanguard S&P Completion	VXF	$953	2	1
Vanguard MSCI Utilities	VPU	$541	1	1

Table A.1 Continued

ETF/ETN Name	Ticker	Net Assets	Share Volume	Ranking
Vanguard MSCI Telecom	VOX	$220	1	1
Vanguard MSCI SmallCap Value	VBR	$1,699	5	1
Vanguard MSCI SmallCap Growth	VBK	$1,472	3	1
Vanguard MSCI SmallCap	VB	$3,988	16	1
Vanguard MSCI MidCap Value	VOE	$735	3	1
Vanguard MSCI MidCap Growth	VOT	$755	1	1
Vanguard MSCI MidCap	VO	$2,681	4	1
Vanguard MSCI Materials	VAW	$510	2	1
Vanguard MSCI LargeCap Value	VTV	$3,656	6	1
Vanguard MSCI LargeCap Growth	VUG	$4,325	10	1
Vanguard MSCI LargeCap	VV	$2,639	5	1
Vanguard MSCI Information Tech	VGT	$1,234	4	1
Vanguard MSCI Industrials	VIS	$348	1	1
Vanguard MSCI Healthcare	VHT	$629	1	1
Vanguard MSCI Energy	VDE	$1,188	3	1
Vanguard MSCI Consumer Staples	VDC	$614	1	1
Vanguard MSCI Consumer Disc.	VCR	$300	2	2
Vanguard Morgan Stanley REIT	VNQ	$6,251	61	3
Vanguard Mergent Dividend	VIG	$2,977	8	3
Vanguard Mega Cap 300 Value	MGV	$228	1	1
Vanguard Mega Cap 300 Growth	MGK	$326	1	2
Vanguard Mega Cap 300	MGC	$248	1	1
Vanguard FTSE High Dividend Yield	VYM	$650	2	2
TDAX Independence in-Target	TDX	$20	0	2
TDAX Independence 2040	TDV	$34	0	2
TDAX Independence 2030	TDN	$35	0	2
TDAX Independence 2020	TDH	$44	0	2
TDAX Independence 2010	TDD	$19	0	2
SPDR Wells Fargo Preferred Stock	PSK	$73	1	1
SPDR Utilities	XLU	$3,209	113	1
SPDR Technology	XLK	$4,480	212	1
SPDR S&P Semiconductor	XSD	$184	4	1
SPDR S&P Retail	XRT	$1,116	336	1
SPDR S&P Pharmaceuticals	XPH	$101	1	1
SPDR S&P Oil & Gas Exploration & Production	XOP	$539	122	1
SPDR S&P Oil & Gas Equipment	XES	$361	5	1
SPDR S&P Metals & Mining	XME	$939	123	1
SPDR S&P Homebuilders	XHB	$997	185	1
SPDR S&P Dividend	SDY	$2,051	10	1
SPDR S&P Biotech	XBI	$559	5	1

(Continued)

Table A.1 Continued

ETF/ETN Name	Ticker	Net Assets	Share Volume	Ranking
SPDR S&P 500	SPY	$74,439	4,119	1
SPDR MS High Tech 35	MTK	$233	1	1
SPDR Materials	XLB	$2,122	211	1
SPDR KBW Regional Bank	KRE	$989	108	1
SPDR KBW Mortgage Finance	KME	$5	0	5
SPDR KBW Insurance	KIE	$285	20	1
SPDR KBW Capital Mkts	KCE	$82	3	1
SPDR KBW Bank	KBE	$993	144	1
SPDR Industrial	XLI	$3,454	322	1
SPDR Health Care	XLV	$2,407	173	1
SPDR Financial	XLF	$7,102	2,711	1
SPDR Energy	XLE	$6,593	446	1
SPDR DJ Total Market	TMW	$195	0	1
SPDR DJ Stoxx 50	FEU	$43	0	1
SPDR DJ SmallCap Val	DSV	$159	1	1
SPDR DJ SmallCap Gr	DSG	$164	0	1
SPDR DJ SmallCap	DSC	$52	0	1
SPDR DJ REIT	RWR	$1,318	9	2
SPDR DJ MidCap Val	EMV	$23	0	1
SPDR DJ MidCap Gr	EMG	$92	0	1
SPDR DJ MidCap	EMM	$54	0	1
SPDR DJ LargeCap Val	ELV	$111	0	1
SPDR DJ LargeCap Gr	ELG	$191	0	1
SPDR DJ LargeCap	ELR	$44	0	1
SPDR Consumer Staples	XLP	$2,268	103	1
SPDR Consumer Discretionary	XLY	$2,279	177	1
Schwab US Small Cap	SCHA	$202	6	1
Schwab US Large Cap Value	SCHV	$57	1	1
Schwab US Large Cap Growth	SCHG	$86	1	1
Schwab US Large Cap	SCHX	$237	6	1
Schwab US Broad Market	SCHB	$240	6	1
Rydex S&P SmallCap Pure Value	RZV	$197	3	1
Rydex S&P SmallCap Pure Growth	RZG	$23	0	1
Rydex S&P Midcap Pure Value	RFV	$73	1	1
Rydex S&P Midcap Pure Growth	RFG	$228	2	1
Rydex S&P LargeCap Pure Value	RPV	$114	3	1
Rydex S&P LargeCap Pure Growth	RPG	$89	1	1
Rydex S&P EW Utilities	RYU	$12	0	1
Rydex S&P EW Technology	RYT	$90	1	1
Rydex S&P EW Materials	RTM	$39	0	1
Rydex S&P EW Industrials	RGI	$42	0	1

Table A.1 Continued

ETF/ETN Name	Ticker	Net Assets	Share Volume	Ranking
Rydex S&P EW Health Care	RYH	$74	0	1
Rydex S&P EW Financials	RYF	$24	0	1
Rydex S&P EW Energy	RYE	$16	0	1
Rydex S&P EW Consumer Staples	RHS	$11	0	1
Rydex S&P EW Consumer Discretionary	RCD	$41	0	1
Rydex S&P 500 EWI	RSP	$2,410	19	1
Rydex Russell 50	XLG	$348	0	1
Rydex 2× S&P Select Sector Technology	RTG	$8	0	5
Rydex 2× S&P Select Sector Health Care	RHM	$3	0	5
Rydex 2× S&P Select Sector Financial	RFL	$22	1	4
Rydex 2× S&P Select Sector Energy	REA	$11	1	4
Rydex 2× S&P Midcap 400	RMM	$22	0	4
Rydex 2× S&P 500	RSU	$111	1	4
Rydex 2× Russell 2000	RRY	$31	1	4
RevenueShares SmallCap	RWJ	$124	1	1
RevenueShares MidCap	RWK	$122	1	1
RevenueShares LargeCap	RWL	$138	1	1
RevenueShares Financials	RWW	$24	1	1
ProShares UltraPro S&P 500	UPRO	$135	32	4
ProShares UltraPro Russell 2000	URTY	$21	5	4
ProShares UltraPro QQQQ	TQQQ	$41	5	4
ProShares UltraPro MidCap 400	UMDD	$26	1	4
ProShares UltraPro Dow30	UDOW	$16	0	4
ProShares Ultra Telecom	LTL	$9	0	5
ProShares Ultra SmallCap 600	SAA	$64	1	1
ProShares Ultra S&P 500	SSO	$1,566	349	4
ProShares Ultra Russell MidCap Value	UVU	$14	1	4
ProShares Ultra Russell MidCap Growth	UKW	$17	0	4
ProShares Ultra Russell 3000	UWC	$7	0	5
ProShares Ultra Russell 2000 Value	UVT	$25	1	4
ProShares Ultra Russell 2000 Growth	UKK	$23	0	4
ProShares Ultra Russell 2000	UWM	$312	53	4
ProShares Ultra Russell 1000 Value	UVG	$16	0	4
ProShares Ultra Russell 1000 Growth	UKF	$19	0	4

(Continued)

Table A.1 Continued

ETF/ETN Name	Ticker	Net Assets	Share Volume	Ranking
ProShares Ultra QQQ	QLD	$837	164	4
ProShares Ultra Nasdaq Biotechnology	BIB	$6	0	5
ProShares Ultra MidCap 400	MVV	$145	3	4
ProShares Ultra KBW Regional Bank	KRU	$6	3	5
ProShares Ultra Dow30	DDM	$375	43	4
ProShares Ultra DJ Utilities	UPW	$23	0	4
ProShares Ultra DJ Technology	ROM	$152	2	4
ProShares Ultra DJ Semiconductors	USD	$95	6	4
ProShares Ultra DJ Real Estate	URE	$682	185	4
ProShares Ultra DJ Oil & Gas	DIG	$369	65	4
ProShares Ultra DJ Industrials	UXI	$43	1	4
ProShares Ultra DJ Health Care	RXL	$34	1	4
ProShares Ultra DJ Financials	UYG	$1,841	190	4
ProShares Ultra DJ Consumer Services	UCC	$23	1	4
ProShares Ultra DJ Consumer Goods	UGE	$30	0	4
ProShares Ultra DJ Basic Materials	UYM	$378	62	4
ProShares Credit Suisse 130/30	CSM	$59	1	5
PowerShares Zacks SmallCap	PZJ	$18	0	1
PowerShares Zacks MicroCap	PZI	$54	1	1
PowerShares Value Line Timeliness & Safety	PIV	$68	1	1
PowerShares Value Line Industry Rotation	PYH	$19	0	3
PowerShares S&P SmallCap Utilities	XLUS	$3	0	5
PowerShares S&P SmallCap Materials	XLBS	$4	0	5
PowerShares S&P SmallCap Information Technology	XLKS	$3	0	5
PowerShares S&P SmallCap Industrials	XLIS	$4	0	5
PowerShares S&P SmallCap Health Care	XLVS	$24	1	1
PowerShares S&P SmallCap Financials	XLFS	$3	0	5
PowerShares S&P SmallCap Energy	XLES	$4	0	5
PowerShares S&P SmallCap Consumer Staples	XLPS	$3	0	5
PowerShares S&P SmallCap Consumer Discretionary	XLYS	$3	0	5
PowerShares S&P 500 BuyWrite	PBP	$168	1	3
PowerShares QQQ	QQQQ	$22,420	1,723	1

Table A.1 Continued

ETF/ETN Name	Ticker	Net Assets	Share Volume	Ranking
PowerShares Preferred	PGX	$1,020	10	2
PowerShares Nasdaq NEXT-Q	PNXQ	$3	0	5
PowerShares Nasdaq Internet	PNQI	$15	0	1
PowerShares Nasdaq 100 BuyWrite	PQBW	$11	0	4
PowerShares Lux Nanotech	PXN	$55	0	1
PowerShares Listed Private Equity	PSP	$212	4	3
PowerShares High Yield Dividend Achievers	PEY	$127	2	1
PowerShares FTSE RAFI 1000	PRF	$646	2	2
PowerShares FTSE NASDAQ Small Cap	PQSC	$1	0	5
PowerShares Financial Preferred	PGF	$1,715	15	1
PowerShares Dynamic Utilities	PUI	$38	0	1
PowerShares Dynamic Telecom & Wireless	PTE	$18	0	1
PowerShares Dynamic Technology	PTF	$39	0	1
PowerShares Dynamic Software	PSJ	$68	1	1
PowerShares Dynamic SmallCap Value	PWY	$72	0	1
PowerShares Dynamic SmallCap Growth	PWT	$32	0	1
PowerShares Dynamic SmallCap	PJM	$19	0	1
PowerShares Dynamic Semiconductors	PSI	$29	0	1
PowerShares Dynamic Retail	PMR	$24	2	1
PowerShares Dynamic Pharmaceuticals	PJP	$58	1	1
PowerShares Dynamic OTC	PWO	$41	0	3
PowerShares Dynamic Oil & Gas	PXJ	$170	2	1
PowerShares Dynamic Networking	PXQ	$48	1	1
PowerShares Dynamic MidCap Value	PWP	$44	0	1
PowerShares Dynamic MidCap Growth	PWJ	$128	1	1
PowerShares Dynamic MidCap	PJG	$25	0	1
PowerShares Dynamic Media	PBS	$126	2	1
PowerShares Dynamic Market	PWC	$230	0	1
PowerShares Dynamic MagniQuant	PIQ	$27	0	4
PowerShares Dynamic Leisure & Ent.	PEJ	$63	3	1
PowerShares Dynamic LargeCap Value	PWV	$349	2	1
PowerShares Dynamic LargeCap Growth	PWB	$230	1	1

(Continued)

Table A.1 Continued

ETF/ETN Name	Ticker	Net Assets	Share Volume	Ranking
PowerShares Dynamic LargeCap	PJF	$38	0	1
PowerShares Dynamic Insurance	PIC	$19	0	1
PowerShares Dynamic Industrials	PRN	$33	0	1
PowerShares Dynamic Health Care Services	PTJ	$22	0	1
PowerShares Dynamic Health Care	PTH	$98	0	1
PowerShares Dynamic Food & Bev	PBJ	$73	1	1
PowerShares Dynamic Financial	PFI	$18	0	1
PowerShares Dynamic Energy Exploration	PXE	$60	0	1
PowerShares Dynamic Energy	PXI	$39	0	1
PowerShares Dynamic Consumer Staples	PSL	$39	0	1
PowerShares Dynamic Consumer Discretionary	PEZ	$21	0	1
PowerShares Dynamic Building & Construction	PKB	$50	1	1
PowerShares Dynamic Biotech	PBE	$214	1	1
PowerShares Dynamic Basic Materials	PYZ	$49	0	1
PowerShares Dynamic Banking	PJB	$25	1	1
PowerShares Dividend Achievers	PFM	$133	1	1
PowerShares Cleantech	PZD	$160	0	1
PowerShares CEF Income Composite	PCEF	$83	2	4
PowerShares Buyback Achievers	PKW	$38	0	1
PowerShares Aerospace & Defense	PPA	$137	1	1
PowerShares Active U.S. Real Estate	PSR	$11	0	1
PowerShares Active Mega-Cap	PMA	$4	0	5
PowerShares Active Alpha Q	PQY	$25	0	5
PowerShares Active Alpha Multi-Cap	PQZ	$3	0	5
MidCap SPDR	MDY	$9,791	71	1
JP Morgan KEYnotes First Trust Enhanced 130/30 LargeCap ETN	JFT	$3	0	5
JP Morgan Alerian MLP ETN	AMJ	$1,254	9	4
JETS Contrarian Opportunities	JCO	$4	0	3
iShares S&P/TOPIX 150	ITF	$122	0	2
iShares S&P US Preferred Stock	PFF	$4,126	20	2
iShares S&P Target Date Retirement Income	TGR	$7	0	5
iShares S&P Target Date 2040	TZV	$10	0	5
iShares S&P Target Date 2035	TZO	$5	0	5
iShares S&P Target Date 2030	TZL	$9	0	5

Table A.1   Continued

ETF/ETN Name	Ticker	Net Assets	Share Volume	Ranking
iShares S&P Target Date 2025	TZI	$9	0	5
iShares S&P Target Date 2020	TZG	$9	0	5
iShares S&P Target Date 2015	TZE	$8	0	5
iShares S&P Target Date 2010	TZD	$6	0	5
iShares S&P SmCap 600 Val	IJS	$2,082	9	1
iShares S&P SmCap 600 Gr	IJT	$1,694	5	1
iShares S&P SmCap 600	IJR	$6,733	33	1
iShares S&P North American Technology	IGM	$459	3	1
iShares S&P North American Software	IGV	$308	1	1
iShares S&P North American Semiconductor	IGW	$287	2	1
iShares S&P North American Networking	IGN	$232	1	1
iShares S&P North American Nat Res	IGE	$1,792	8	1
iShares S&P New York Muni	NYF	$68	0	3
iShares S&P Moderate Allocation	AOM	$54	0	2
iShares S&P MdCap 400 Val	IJJ	$2,242	7	1
iShares S&P MdCap 400 Gr	IJK	$2,921	7	1
iShares S&P MdCap 400	IJH	$8,049	20	1
iShares S&P Growth Allocation	AOR	$57	0	1
iShares S&P Conservative Allocation	AOK	$35	0	2
iShares S&P Aggressive Allocation	AOA	$46	0	2
iShares S&P 500 Val	IVE	$4,148	11	1
iShares S&P 500 Gr	IVW	$5,628	15	1
iShares S&P 500	IVV	$23,115	75	1
iShares S&P 1500	ISI	$320	0	1
iShares S&P 100	OEF	$2,568	14	1
iShares Russell Top 200 Value	IWX	$171	1	1
iShares Russell Top 200 Growth	IWY	$173	1	1
iShares Russell Top 200	IWL	$7	0	5
iShares Russell Midcap Val	IWS	$3,003	27	1
iShares Russell Midcap Gr	IWP	$3,400	16	1
iShares Russell Midcap	IWR	$5,757	21	1
iShares Russell MicroCap	IWC	$434	6	1
iShares Russell 3000 Val	IWW	$371	2	1
iShares Russell 3000 Gr	IWZ	$317	1	2
iShares Russell 3000	IWV	$3,150	14	1
iShares Russell 2000 Val	IWN	$4,786	49	1

(Continued)

Table A.1 Continued

ETF/ETN Name	Ticker	Net Assets	Share Volume	Ranking
iShares Russell 2000 Gr	IWO	$3,342	57	1
iShares Russell 2000	IWM	$14,401	1,433	1
iShares Russell 1000 Val	IWD	$9,661	40	1
iShares Russell 1000 Gr	IWF	$11,640	63	1
iShares Russell 1000	IWB	$5,596	36	1
iShares NYSE Composite	NYC	$113	0	1
iShares NYSE 100	NY	$66	0	1
iShares Nasdaq Biotech	IBB	$1,544	16	1
iShares MSCI-Chile	ECH	$346	3	3
iShares Morningstar Small Value	JKL	$195	1	1
iShares Morningstar Small Growth	JKK	$91	0	1
iShares Morningstar Small Core	JKJ	$180	0	1
iShares Morningstar Mid Value	JKI	$136	0	1
iShares Morningstar Mid Growth	JKH	$169	1	1
iShares Morningstar Mid Core	JKG	$126	0	1
iShares Morningstar Large Value	JKF	$213	0	1
iShares Morningstar Large Growth	JKE	$447	1	1
iShares Morningstar Large Core	JKD	$266	0	1
iShares KLD Select Social SM	KLD	$132	0	1
iShares KLD 400 Social Index	DSI	$118	0	1
iShares FTSE NAREIT Retail	RTL	$11	0	1
iShares FTSE NAREIT Residential Plus	REZ	$45	0	1
iShares FTSE NAREIT Real Estate 50	FTY	$43	1	1
iShares FTSE NAREIT Mortgage Plus	REM	$58	1	1
iShares FTSE NAREIT Industrial/ Office	FIO	$10	0	5
iShares FTSE EPRA/NAREIT North America	IFNA	$8	0	5
iShares DJ Utilities	IDU	$469	1	1
iShares DJ U.S. Telecom	IYZ	$584	10	1
iShares DJ U.S. Technology	IYW	$1,421	8	1
iShares DJ U.S. Select Dividend	DVY	$4,340	9	1
iShares DJ U.S. Regional Bank	IAT	$203	4	1
iShares DJ U.S. Real Estate	IYR	$3,159	357	1
iShares DJ U.S. Pharmaceutical	IHE	$171	1	1
iShares DJ U.S. Oil Equip/Svc	IEZ	$413	6	1
iShares DJ U.S. Oil & Gas Exploration	IEO	$425	11	1
iShares DJ U.S. Medical Devices	IHI	$446	2	1

Table A.1 Continued

ETF/ETN Name	Ticker	Net Assets	Share Volume	Ranking
iShares DJ U.S. Insurance	IAK	$85	1	1
iShares DJ U.S. Industrial	IYJ	$366	2	1
iShares DJ U.S. Index	IYY	$598	1	1
iShares DJ U.S. Home Construction	ITB	$344	18	1
iShares DJ U.S. Healthcare	IYH	$722	2	1
iShares DJ U.S. Healthcare	IHF	$198	2	1
iShares DJ U.S. Financial Svcs	IYG	$345	6	1
iShares DJ U.S. Financial	IYF	$565	54	1
iShares DJ U.S. Energy	IYE	$745	7	1
iShares DJ U.S. Consumer Svcs	IYC	$196	2	1
iShares DJ U.S. Cons Goods	IYK	$354	3	1
iShares DJ U.S. Broker–Dealer	IAI	$108	4	1
iShares DJ U.S. Basic Materials	IYM	$784	29	1
iShares DJ U.S. Aerospace & Defense	ITA	$239	2	1
iShares DJ Transportation	IYT	$547	19	1
iShares Cohen & Steers Realty	ICF	$2,154	22	2
iPath S&P 500 VIX Short Term Futures ETN	VXX	$1,581	283	5
iPath S&P 500 VIX Mid Term Futures ETN	VXZ	$956	9	5
iPath DJ AIG Industrial ETN	JJM	$65	1	4
iPath CBOE S&P 500 BuyWrite ETN	BWV	$16	0	4
IndexIQ Hedge Multi Strategy	QAI	$93	1	5
IndexIQ Hedge Macro	MCRO	$11	0	4
IndexIQ ARB Merger Arb	MNA	$32	1	2
HOLDRs Pharmaceutical	PPH	$615	11	1
HOLDRs Market 2000+	MKH	$22	0	1
HOLDRs Internet Infrastr	IIH	$9	2	5
HOLDRs Internet Arch	IAH	$51	0	1
HOLDRs Internet	HHH	$129	1	1
HOLDRs Broadband	BDH	$16	0	1
HOLDRs Biotech	BBH	$330	1	1
HOLDRs B2B Internet	BHH	$2	1	5
Grail RP Technology	RPQ	$4	0	5
Grail RP Growth	RPX	$4	0	5
Grail RP Focused LargeCap Growth	RWG	$7	0	5
Grail RP Financials	RFF	$3	0	5
Grail American Beacon Large Cap Value	GVT	$3	0	5
Geary Advisors TXF Large Companies	TXF	$6	0	5

(Continued)

Table A.1 Continued

ETF/ETN Name	Ticker	Net Assets	Share Volume	Ranking
Geary Advisors Ook Inc.	OOK	$4	0	5
First Trust Value Line Equity Allocation	FVI	$11	0	2
First Trust Value Line Dividend	FVD	$165	1	1
First Trust Value Line 100	FVL	$64	0	1
First Trust Utilities AlphaDEX	FXU	$32	0	1
First Trust Technology AlphaDEX	FXL	$56	1	1
First Trust Small Cap Core AlphaDEX	FYX	$41	1	1
First Trust S&P REIT	FRI	$63	2	1
First Trust NYSEArca Biotech	FBT	$179	3	1
First Trust Nasdaq Clean Edge Smart Grid Infrastructure	GRID	$33	0	1
First Trust Nasdaq Clean Edge Green Energy	QCLN	$40	0	1
First Trust Nasdaq ABA Community Bank	QABA	$9	0	5
First Trust Nasdaq 100 Tech	QTEC	$203	3	1
First Trust Nasdaq 100 ex-Tech	QQXT	$20	0	1
First Trust Nasdaq 100 EWI	QQEW	$66	0	1
First Trust Multi Cap Value AlphaDEX	FAB	$28	0	1
First Trust Multi Cap Growth AlphaDEX	FAD	$8	0	5
First Trust Morningstar Dividend Leaders	FDL	$53	0	1
First Trust Mid Cap Core AlphaDEX	FNX	$63	1	1
First Trust Materials AlphaDEX	FXZ	$200	3	1
First Trust Large Cap Value AlphaDEX	FTA	$49	0	1
First Trust Large Cap Growth AlphaDEX	FTC	$30	0	1
First Trust Large Cap Core AlphaDEX	FEX	$52	1	1
First Trust ISE Revere Natural Gas	FCG	$444	20	1
First Trust IPOX 100	FPX	$11	0	1
First Trust Industrials AlphaDEX	FXR	$31	0	1
First Trust Health Care AlphaDEX	FXH	$60	1	1
First Trust Financials AlphaDEX	FXO	$137	4	1
First Trust Energy AlphaDEX	FXN	$63	1	1
First Trust DJ STOXX Select Dividend 30	FDD	$7	0	5

Table A.1   Continued

ETF/ETN Name	Ticker	Net Assets	Share Volume	Ranking
First Trust DJ MicroCap	FDM	$22	0	1
First Trust DJ Internet	FDN	$215	3	1
First Trust DB Strategic Value	FDV	$45	0	2.
First Trust Consumer Staples AlphaDEX	FXG	$28	0	1
First Trust Consumer Discretionary AlphaDEX	FXD	$159	4	1
Fidelity NASDAQ Composite	ONEQ	$165	1	2
FaithShares Methodist Values	FMV	$3	0	5
FaithShares Lutheran Values	FKL	$3	0	5
FaithShares Christian Values	FOC	$3	0	5
FaithShares Catholic Values	FCV	$3	0	5
FaithShares Baptist Values	FZB	$3	0	5
E-TRACS UBS Alerian MLP Infrastructure ETN	MLPI	$30	1	4
Elements SPECTRUM LargeCap Sector Momentum ETN	EEH	$1	0	5
Elements Morningstar Wide Moats Focus ETN	WMW	$8	0	5
Elements Dogs of the Dow ETN	DOD	$2	0	5
Elements Benjamin Graham Total Mkt Value ETN	BVT	$1	0	5
Elements Benjamin Graham Small Cap Value ETN	BSC	$4	0	5
Elements Benjamin Graham Large Cap Value ETN	BVL	$1	0	5
Direxion Daily Technology Bull 3×	TYH	$189	9	4
Direxion Daily SmallCap Bull 3×	TNA	$324	160	4
Direxion Daily Semiconductor Bull 3×	SOXL	$22	2	4
Direxion Daily Semiconductor Bear 3×	SOXS	$3	0	5
Direxion Daily Real Estate Bull 3×	DRN	$118	15	4
Direxion Daily MidCap Bull 3×	MWJ	$45	2	4
Direxion Daily LargeCap Bull 3×	BGU	$212	88	4
Direxion Daily Financials Bull 3×	FAS	$1,113	578	4
Direxion Daily Energy Bull 3×	ERX	$148	69	4
Diamonds DJIA	DIA	$9,073	213	1
Credit Suisse Long/Short Liquid Index ETN	CSLS	$16	0	5

(Continued)

Table A.1 Continued

ETF/ETN Name	Ticker	Net Assets	Share Volume	Ranking
Claymore/Zacks Sector Rotation	XRO	$23	0	5
Claymore/Zacks Multi Asset Income	CVY	$239	3	3
Claymore/Zacks MidCap Core	CZA	$7	0	5
Claymore/Sabrient Stealth	STH	$3	0	5
Claymore/Sabrient Insider	NFO	$138	1	2
Claymore/Sabrient Defensive Equity	DEF	$14	0	2
Claymore/Raymond James SB-1 Equity	RYJ	$64	0	2
Claymore/NYSEArca Airline	FAA	$42	1	1
Claymore/Beacon Spin Off	CSD	$18	0	3
Claymore Wilshire US REIT	WREI	$1	0	5
Claymore Wilshire 5000	WFVK	$3	0	5
Claymore Wilshire 4500	WXSP	$5	0	5
Claymore CEF Index Linked GS Connect ETN	GCE	$3	0	5
Barclays Long C Leveraged S&P 500 ETN	BXUC	$11	0	4
Barclays Long B Leveraged S&P 500 ETN	BXUB	$6	0	5
ALPS Equal Sector Weight	EQL	$31	0	1
AdvisorShares Dent Tactical	DENT	$28	0	5
Global Equity Short				
ProShares UltraShort MSCI Pacific ex-Japan	JPX	$3	0	5
ProShares UltraShort MSCI Mexico	SMK	$3	0	5
ProShares UltraShort MSCI Japan	EWV	$13	0	4
ProShares UltraShort MSCI Europe	EPV	$48	4	4
ProShares UltraShort MSCI Emerging Mkts	EEV	$176	37	4
ProShares UltraShort MSCI EAFE	EFU	$31	1	4
ProShares UltraShort MSCI Brazil	BZQ	$30	2	4
ProShares UltraShort MidCap 400	MZZ	$40	4	4
ProShares UltraShort FTSE/Xinhua China 25	FXP	$441	79	4
ProShares Short MSCI Emerging Mkts	EUM	$238	2	4
ProShares Short MSCI EAFE	EFZ	$57	1	4
ProShares Short FTSE/Xinhua 25	YXI	$5	0	5
Direxion Daily India Bear 3×	INDZ	$4	0	5
Direxion Daily Em Mkts Bear 3×	EDZ	$168	40	4
Direxion Daily Dev Mkts Bear 3×	DPK	$10	2	5
Direxion Daily China Bear 3×	CZI	$10	0	5

Table A.1 Continued

ETF/ETN Name	Ticker	Net Assets	Share Volume	Ranking
Direxion Daily BRIC Bear 3×	BRIS	$4	0	5
Global Equity Long				
WisdomTree World ex-US Growth	DNL	$30	0	2
WisdomTree Pacific ex-Japan Total Dividend	DND	$90	0	2
WisdomTree Pacific ex-Japan Equity Income	DNH	$108	1	2
WisdomTree Middle East Dividend	GULF	$16	0	3
WisdomTree Japan Total Dividend	DXJ	$92	2	2
WisdomTree Japan Small Cap Dividend	DFJ	$173	1	2
WisdomTree Int'l Utilities	DBU	$47	1	2
WisdomTree Int'l Small Cap Dividend	DLS	$445	1	3
WisdomTree Int'l Real Estate	DRW	$84	1	2
WisdomTree Int'l Mid Cap Dividend	DIM	$146	0	2
WisdomTree Int'l Large Cap Dividend	DOL	$146	0	2
WisdomTree Int'l Hedged Equity	HEDJ	$14	0	3
WisdomTree Int'l Energy	DKA	$46	1	2
WisdomTree Int'l Dividend ex-Financials	DOO	$163	0	2
WisdomTree Int'l Basic Materials	DBN	$48	0	2
WisdomTree India Earnings	EPI	$882	25	2
WisdomTree Europe Small Cap Dividend	DFE	$31	0	2
WisdomTree Equity Income	DHS	$124	0	1
WisdomTree EM Small Cap Dividend	DGS	$409	4	2
WisdomTree EM Equity Income	DEM	$585	3	2
WisdomTree DEFA High Yield Equity	DTH	$139	1	2
WisdomTree DEFA	DWM	$437	1	2
Vanguard MSCI Total Market	VTI	$14,961	31	1
Vanguard MSCI Pacific	VPL	$1,476	3	1
Vanguard MSCI Financials	VFH	$569	5	2
Vanguard MSCI Europe Pacific	VEA	$4,415	33	2
Vanguard MSCI Europe	VGK	$2,560	18	1
Vanguard MSCI Emerging Markets	VWO	$24,447	325	2
Vanguard FTSE Total World Stock	VT	$682	3	2
Vanguard FTSE All World ex-U.S. Small Cap	VSS	$503	1	2
Vanguard FTSE All World ex-U.S.	VEU	$5,616	23	2
Vanguard Extended Duration Treasury	EDV	$85	0	3

(Continued)

Table A.1 Continued

ETF/ETN Name	Ticker	Net Assets	Share Volume	Ranking
SPDR S&P World ex-U.S. Small Cap	GWX	$658	4	2
SPDR S&P World ex-U.S.	GWL	$106	1	2
SPDR S&P Russia	RBL	$5	0	5
SPDR S&P Middle East & Africa	GAF	$134	1	3
SPDR S&P Latin America	GML	$200	1	2
SPDR S&P Int'l Utilities	IPU	$8	0	5
SPDR S&P Int'l Telecom	IST	$15	0	2
SPDR S&P Int'l Technology	IPK	$23	0	2
SPDR S&P Int'l Mid Cap	MDD	$27	0	2
SPDR S&P Int'l Materials	IRV	$19	0	2
SPDR S&P Int'l Industrial	IPN	$10	0	5
SPDR S&P Int'l Health Care	IRY	$7	0	5
SPDR S&P Int'l Financials	IPF	$11	0	2
SPDR S&P Int'l Energy	IPW	$12	0	2
SPDR S&P Int'l Dividend	DWX	$219	1	2
SPDR S&P Int'l Consumer Staples	IPS	$8	0	5
SPDR S&P Int'l Consumer Disc	IPD	$9	0	5
SPDR S&P European Emerging Mkt	GUR	$264	3	2
SPDR S&P Emerging Markets Small Cap	EWX	$272	5	2
SPDR S&P Emerging Markets	GMM	$152	1	2
SPDR S&P China	GXC	$562	2	2
SPDR S&P BRIC 40	BIK	$446	3	2
SPDR S&P Asia Pacific Emerging Mkt	GMF	$651	2	2
SPDR Russell/Nomura Small Cap Japan	JSC	$83	0	2
SPDR Russell/Nomura Prime Japan	JPP	$16	0	2
SPDR MSCI ACWI ex-US	CWI	$401	1	2
SPDR FTSE/Macquarie Global Infrastructure 100	GII	$57	0	2
SPDR DJ Int'l Real Estate	RWX	$1,166	3	1
SPDR DJ Global Titans	DGT	$96	0	2
SPDR DJ Global REIT	RWO	$129	0	2
SPDR DJ EuroStoxx 50	FEZ	$142	1	2
Schwab Int'l Small Cap	SCHC	$43	1	1
Schwab Int'l Equity	SCHF	$234	5	2
Schwab Emerging Mkts	SCHE	$98	2	2
RevenueShares Navellier Overall A-100	RWV	$12	0	3
RevenueShares ADR	RTR	$54	0	2

Table A.1 Continued

ETF/ETN Name	Ticker	Net Assets	Share Volume	Ranking
ProShares Ultra MSCI Pacific ex-Japan	UXJ	$3	0	5
ProShares Ultra MSCI Mexico	UMX	$3	0	5
ProShares Ultra MSCI Japan	EZJ	$11	0	4
ProShares Ultra MSCI Europe	UPV	$3	0	5
ProShares Ultra MSCI Emerging Mkts	EET	$31	1	4
ProShares Ultra MSCI EAFE	EFO	$7	0	5
ProShares Ultra MSCI Brazil	UBR	$3	0	5
ProShares Ultra FTSE/Xinhua 25	XPP	$43	1	4
PowerShares WilderHill Progressive Energy	PUW	$60	0	2
PowerShares WilderHill Clean Energy	PBW	$658	9	2
PowerShares Water	PHO	$1,335	6	2
PowerShares USX China	PGJ	$456	2	2
PowerShares MENA Frontier Countries	PMNA	$16	0	3
PowerShares Int'l Dividend	PID	$428	5	2
PowerShares India	PIN	$423	8	2
PowerShares Global Wind Energy	PWND	$36	0	2
PowerShares Global Water	PIO	$338	2	2
PowerShares Global Steel	PSTL	$12	0	2
PowerShares Global Progressive Transportation	PTRP	$6	0	5
PowerShares Global Nuclear Energy	PKN	$39	1	2
PowerShares Global Gold and Precious Metals	PSAU	$43	0	2
PowerShares Global Coal	PKOL	$16	0	2
PowerShares Global Clean Energy	PBD	$187	1	1
PowerShares Global Biotech	PBTQ	$4	0	5
PowerShares Global Agriculture	PAGG	$64	1	2
PowerShares FTSE RAFI US 1500 Small–Mid	PRFZ	$284	1	1
PowerShares FTSE RAFI Japan	PJO	$8	0	5
PowerShares FTSE RAFI Europe	PEF	$15	0	2
PowerShares FTSE RAFI Emerging Mkts	PXH	$324	2	2
PowerShares FTSE RAFI Developed Markets ex-US Small Mid	PDN	$46	0	2
PowerShares FTSE RAFI Developed Markets ex-US	PXF	$163	1	2

(Continued)

Table A.1 Continued

ETF/ETN Name	Ticker	Net Assets	Share Volume	Ranking
PowerShares FTSE RAFI Asia Pacific ex-Japan	PAF	$46	0	2
PowerShares Emerging Mkts Infrastructure	PXR	$146	1	2
PowerShares Dynamic Developed Intl Opportunities	PFA	$41	0	2
PowerShares DWA Technical Leaders	PDP	$159	1	1
PowerShares DWA Emerging Mkts Technical	PIE	$69	5	2
PowerShares DWA Developed Mkts Technical	PIZ	$34	1	2
PowerShares BLDRs Europe 100	ADRU	$20	0	2
PowerShares BLDRs Emerging Mkts 50	ADRE	$694	2	2
PowerShares BLDRs Developed Mkts 100	ADRD	$77	0	2
PowerShares BLDRs Asia 50	ADRA	$54	0	2
PowerShares Autonomic Growth NFA Global Asset	PTO	$11	0	2
PowerShares Autonomic Balanced NFA Global Asset	PCA	$13	0	3
PowerShares Autonomic Balanced Growth NFA Global Asset	PAO	$10	0	5
Market Vectors Vietnam	VNM	$143	3	3
Market Vectors Solar Energy	KWT	$30	1	2
Market Vectors RVE Hard Assets Producers	HAP	$102	1	2
Market Vectors Russia	RSX	$1,991	72	3
Market Vectors Poland	PLND	$20	1	3
Market Vectors Nuclear Energy	NLR	$185	1	2
Market Vectors Latin America Small Cap	LATM	$4	0	2
Market Vectors Junior Gold Miners	GDXJ	$1,155	38	3
Market Vectors Indonesia	IDX	$386	3	3
Market Vectors Gulf States	MES	$12	0	3
Market Vectors Gold Miners	GDX	$6,401	226	2
Market Vectors Global Alternative Energy	GEX	$190	1	2
Market Vectors Gaming	BJK	$121	0	2
Market Vectors Environmental Services	EVX	$25	0	2

Table A.1 Continued

ETF/ETN Name	Ticker	Net Assets	Share Volume	Ranking
Market Vectors Egypt	EGPT	$3	0	5
Market Vectors Coal	KOL	$403	7	1
Market Vectors Brazil Small Cap	BRF	$716	8	2
Market Vectors Agribusiness	MOO	$1,934	17	2
Market Vectors Africa	AFK	$63	1	3
JETS DJ Islamic	JVS	$2	0	5
iShares S&P Latin America 40	ILF	$2,701	57	2
iShares S&P India Nifty 50	INDY	$60	1	2
iShares S&P Global Utilities	JXI	$249	1	2
iShares S&P Global Timber	WOOD	$58	1	2
iShares S&P Global Telecom	IXP	$306	2	1
iShares S&P Global Tech	IXN	$564	2	2
iShares S&P Global Nuclear	NUCL	$18	0	2
iShares S&P Global Materials	MXI	$905	2	2
iShares S&P Global Infrastructure	IGF	$475	2	1
iShares S&P Global Industrials	EXI	$203	1	2
iShares S&P Global Healthcare	IXJ	$570	1	2
iShares S&P Global Financials	IXG	$319	1	2
iShares S&P Global Energy	IXC	$1,100	3	2
iShares S&P Global EM Infrastructure	EMIF	$50	1	2
iShares S&P Global Consumer Staples	KXI	$342	1	2
iShares S&P Global Consumer Disc	RXI	$97	0	2
iShares S&P Global Clean Energy	ICLN	$65	1	2
iShares S&P Global 100	IOO	$833	2	2
iShares S&P Europe 350	IEV	$1,367	9	2
iShares S&P Developed ex-U.S. Property	WPS	$112	0	2
iShares S&P Asia 50	AIA	$156	1	1
iShares MSCI—UK	EWU	$1,067	34	2
iShares MSCI—Turkey	TUR	$523	5	3
iShares MSCI—Thailand	THD	$320	9	3
iShares MSCI—Taiwan	EWT	$3,416	352	2
iShares MSCI—Switzerland	EWL	$380	7	2
iShares MSCI—Sweden	EWD	$226	6	2
iShares MSCI—Spain	EWP	$189	7	2
iShares MSCI—South Korea	EWY	$3,741	78	2
iShares MSCI—South Africa	EZA	$514	7	3
iShares MSCI—Singapore	EWS	$1,534	70	2
iShares MSCI—Pacific ex-Japan	EPP	$4,006	28	2
iShares MSCI—Netherlands	EWN	$133	3	2

(Continued)

Table A.1 Continued

ETF/ETN Name	Ticker	Net Assets	Share Volume	Ranking
iShares MSCI—Mexico	EWW	**$1,520**	81	2
iShares MSCI—Malaysia	EWM	**$649**	31	3
iShares MSCI—Kokusai	TOK	**$256**	2	2
iShares MSCI—Japan Small Cap	SCJ	**$40**	0	2
iShares MSCI—Japan	EWJ	**$5,570**	554	2
iShares MSCI—Italy	EWI	**$107**	4	2
iShares MSCI—Israel	EIS	**$251**	2	3
iShares MSCI—Hong Kong	EWH	**$1,954**	119	2
iShares MSCI—Germany	EWG	**$897**	35	2
iShares MSCI—France	EWQ	**$295**	8	2
iShares MSCI—Far East Financials	FEFN	**$3**	0	5
iShares MSCI—Europe Financials	EUFN	**$2**	0	5
iShares MSCI—EMU	EZU	**$703**	9	2
iShares MSCI—Emerging Mkts Materials	EMMT	**$5**	0	5
iShares MSCI—Emerging Mkts Financials	EMFN	**$3**	0	5
iShares MSCI—Emerging Mkts Eastern Europe	ESR	**$14**	0	3
iShares MSCI—Emerging Mkts	EEM	**$35,750**	1,507	2
iShares MSCI—EAFE Value	EFV	**$1,349**	3	2
iShares MSCI—EAFE Small Cap	SCZ	**$991**	8	2
iShares MSCI—EAFE Growth	EFG	**$1,356**	2	2
iShares MSCI—EAFE	EFA	**$35,813**	430	2
iShares MSCI—Canada	EWC	**$3,763**	72	2
iShares MSCI—BRIC	BKF	**$980**	6	2
iShares MSCI—Brazil	EWZ	**$10,814**	399	2
iShares MSCI—Belgium	EWK	**$64**	6	2
iShares MSCI—Austria	EWO	**$135**	5	2
iShares MSCI—Australia	EWA	**$2,818**	88	2
iShares MSCI Peru	EPU	**$189**	4	3
iShares MSCI All Country ex-Japan	AAXJ	**$1,528**	8	2
iShares MSCI ACWI ex-U.S. Financials	AXFN	**$2**	0	5
iShares MSCI ACWI ex-U.S.	ACWX	**$666**	4	2
iShares MSCI ACWI	ACWI	**$1,146**	6	2
iShares FTSE/XINHUA China 25	FXI	**$8,332**	598	2
iShares FTSE EPRA/NAREIT Global Real Estate ex-U.S.	IFGL	**$325**	2	2
iShares FTSE EPRA/NAREIT Europe	IFEU	**$8**	0	5

Table A.1 Continued

ETF/ETN Name	Ticker	Net Assets	Share Volume	Ranking
iShares FTSE EPRA/NAREIT Asia	IFAS	$23	0	2
iShares FTSE Dev Small Cap ex-North American	IFSM	$35	0	2
iShares FTSE China HK Listed	FCHI	$58	0	2
iShares Dow Jones EPAC Select Dividend	IDV	$130	1	2
iShares Diversified Alternatives	ALT	$55	0	4
iPath MSCI India ETN	INP	$1,073	8	4
iPath Global Carbon ETN	GRN	$3	0	5
IndexIQ South Korea Small Cap	SKOR	$3	0	5
IndexIQ Canada Small Cap	CNDA	$9	0	5
IndexIQ Australia Small Cap	KROO	$9	0	5
IndexIQ ARB Global Resources	GRES	$8	0	5
HOLDRs Wireless	WMH	$20	0	1
HOLDRs Utiliites	UTH	$99	0	1
HOLDRs Telecom	TTH	$127	2	1
HOLDRs Software	SWH	$79	1	1
HOLDRs Semiconductor	SMH	$749	305	1
HOLDRs Retail	RTH	$476	47	1
HOLDRs Regional Bank	RKH	$200	13	1
HOLDRs Europe 2001	EKH	$6	0	5
GlobalX/Interbolsa FTSE Columbia 20	GXG	$10	0	5
GlobalX/FTSE Nordic 30	GXF	$6	0	5
GlobalX Silver Miners	SIL	$2	4	5
GlobalX Copper Miners	COPX	$2	0	5
GlobalX China Technology	CHIB	$4	0	5
GlobalX China Materials	CHIM	$14	0	2
GlobalX China Industrial	CHII	$25	0	2
GlobalX China Financial	CHIX	$54	1	2
GlobalX China Energy	CHIE	$4	0	5
GlobalX China Consumer	CHIQ	$31	1	2
GlobalShares FTSE Emerging Markets	GSR	$67	0	2
GlobalShares FTSE Developed ex-U.S.	GSD	$13	0	2
GlobalShares FTSE All World ex-U.S.	GSO	$6	0	5
GlobalShares FTSE All World	GSW	$4	0	5
GlobalShares FTSE All Cap Asia Pacific ex-Japan	GSZ	$6	0	5

(Continued)

Table A.1   Continued

ETF/ETN Name	Ticker	Net Assets	Share Volume	Ranking
First Trust ISE Water	FIW	$46	1	2
First Trust ISE Global Wind	FAN	$68	1	2
First Trust ISE Global Platinum	PLTM	$6	0	5
First Trust ISE Global Engineering & Construction	FLM	$42	0	2
First Trust ISE Global Copper	CU	$5	0	5
First Trust ISE Chindia	FNI	$148	1	2
First Trust FTSE/EPRA NAREIT Global Real Estate	FFR	$37	0	2
First Trust DJ Global Select Dividend	FGD	$27	0	2
First Trust BICK	BICK	$7	0	5
Emerging Global INDXX China Infrastructure	CHXX	$7	0	5
Emerging Global INDXX Brazil Infrastructure	BRXX	$22	1	3
Emerging Global DJ Emerging Mkt Titans	EEG	$37	0	2
Emerging Global DJ Emerging Mkt Metals & Mining	EMT	$28	0	2
Emerging Global DJ Emerging Mkt Financials	EFN	$12	0	2
Emerging Global DJ Emerging Mkt Energy	EEO	$10	0	5
Elements S&P Commodity Trends Indicator Total Return ETN	LSC	$71	2	4
Elements CS Global Warming ETN	GWO	$3	0	5
Direxion Daily Latin America Bull 3×	LBJ	$26	2	4
Direxion Daily Latin America Bear 3×	LHB	$6	0	5
Direxion Daily India Bull 3×	INDL	$6	0	5
Direxion Daily Em Mkts Bull 3×	EDC	$317	23	4
Direxion Daily Dev Mkts Bull 3×	DZK	$20	0	4
Direxion Daily China Bull 3×	CZM	$26	1	4
Direxion Daily BRIC Bull 3×	BRIL	$4	0	5
Credit Suisse Cushing 30 MLP ETN	MLPN	$33	2	4
Claymore/Zacks International Multi Asset Income	HGI	$61	0	2
Claymore/Zacks Dividend Rotation	IRO	$9	0	5
Claymore/Zacks Country Rotation	CRO	$7	0	5
Claymore/SWM Canadian Energy	ENY	$87	1	2

Table A.1 Continued

ETF/ETN Name	Ticker	Net Assets	Share Volume	Ranking
Claymore/S&P Global Dividend Opportunities	LVL	$14	0	2
Claymore/Robb Report Global Luxury	ROB	$17	0	1
Claymore/Ocean Tomo Patent	OTP	$17	0	3
Claymore/Ocean Tomo Growth	OTR	$8	0	5
Claymore/MAC Global Solar Energy	TAN	$174	10	2
Claymore/BNY Mellon Intl Small Cap LDRS	XGC	$6	0	5
Claymore/BNY Mellon Frontier Markets	FRN	$34	0	3
Claymore/BNY Mellon Euro-Pacific LDRs	EEN	$5	0	5
Claymore/BNY Mellon BRIC	EEB	$1,037	6	2
Claymore/Beacon Global Timber	CUT	$147	5	2
Claymore/Beacon Global Exchanges, Brokers, Asset Mgrs	EXB	$3	0	5
Claymore/AlphaShares China Small Cap	HAO	$356	7	2
Claymore/AlphaShares China Real Estate	TAO	$55	1	2
Claymore/AlphaShares China All Cap	YAO	$78	1	2
Claymore S&P Global Water	CGW	$248	1	2
Claymore China Technology	CQQQ	$27	1	2
Barclays GEMS ETN	JEM	$4	0	5
Barclays GEMS Asia 8 ETN	AYT	$3	0	5
Barclays Asian & Gulf Currency Revaluation ETN	PGD	$7	0	5
ALPS TR/J CRB Wildcatters Exploration & Dev	WCAT	$4	0	5
ALPS Thomson Reuters/Jefferies CRB Industrial Metals Equity	CRBI	$6	0	5
ALPS Thomson Reuters/Jefferies CRB Commodity Equity	CRBQ	$78	0	2
ALPS Thomson Reuters/Jefferies CRB Agriculture Equity	CRBA	$4	0	5
ALPS Cohen & Steers Global Realty	GRI	$25	0	2
Wisdom Tree Global Equity Income	DEW	$49	0	2

(Continued)

Table A.1   Continued

ETF/ETN Name	Ticker	Net Assets	Share Volume	Ranking
Fixed Income Short				
ProShares UltraShort Lehman 7–10 Year	PST	$391	4	4
ProShares UltraShort Lehman 20+ Year	TBT	$5,118	200	3
ProShares Short 20+ Year Treasury	TBF	$505	6	4
Direxion Daily 30 Yr Treasury Bear 3×	TMV	$174	4	4
Direxion Daily 2 Yr Treasury Bear 3×	TWOZ	$10	0	5
Direxion Daily 10 Yr Treasury Bear 3×	TYO	$35	0	4
Fixed Income Long				
Vanguard Barclays Total Bond	BND	$7,271	12	3
Vanguard Barclays Short Term Govt Bond	VGSH	$36	0	3
Vanguard Barclays Short Term Corp Bond	VCSH	$374	2	3
Vanguard Barclays Short Term Bond	BSV	$4,520	11	3
Vanguard Barclays Mortgage Backed Securities	VMBS	$45	0	3
Vanguard Barclays Long Term Govt Bond	VGLT	$18	0	3
Vanguard Barclays Long Term Corp Bond	VCLT	$38	0	3
Vanguard Barclays Long Term Bond	BLV	$353	1	3
Vanguard Barclays Intermediate Term Govt Bond	VGIT	$21	0	3
Vanguard Barclays Intermediate Term Corp Bond	VCIT	$161	1	3
Vanguard Barclays Intermediate Term Bond	BIV	$1,507	3	3
SPDR S&P VRDO Muni	VRD	$15	0	3
SPDR DB Int'l Gov't Inflation Protected Bond	WIP	$1,006	2	3
SPDR Barcap TIPS	IPE	$387	1	2
SPDR Barcap Short Term Muni	SHM	$1,137	9	3
SPDR Barcap Short Term Int'l Treasury	BWZ	$144	1	3
SPDR Barcap Short Term Corp Bond	SCPB	$129	2	3

Table A.1   Continued

ETF/ETN Name	Ticker	Net Assets	Share Volume	Ranking
SPDR Barcap NY Muni	INY	$25	0	3
SPDR Barcap Muni	TFI	$894	5	3
SPDR Barcap Mortgage Backed	MBG	$13	0	3
SPDR Barcap Long Term Treasury	TLO	$22	0	3
SPDR Barcap Long Term Credit	LWC	$29	0	3
SPDR Barcap Int'l Treasury	BWX	$1,105	4	3
SPDR Barcap Intermediate Term Treasury	ITE	$214	1	3
SPDR Barcap Intermediate Term Credit	ITR	$97	1	3
SPDR Barcap High Yield Bond	JNK	$4,560	42	3
SPDR Barcap Convertible Bond	CWB	$310	2	3
SPDR Barcap CA Muni	CXA	$63	0	3
SPDR Barcap Agg	LAG	$217	1	3
SPDR Barcap 1–3 Month Bill	BIL	$779	11	3
ProShares Ultra 7–10 Year Treasury	UST	$15	0	3
ProShares Ultra 20+ Year Treasury	UBT	$7	1	5
PowerShares VRDO Tax Free Weekly	PVI	$840	9	1
PowerShares Insured NY Muni	PZT	$37	0	3
PowerShares Insured National Muni	PZA	$522	3	3
PowerShares Insured CA Muni	PWZ	$39	0	3
PowerShares High Yield Corporate Bond	PHB	$224	3	3
PowerShares Emerging Mkts Sovereign Debt	PCY	$594	7	3
PowerShares Build America Bond	BAB	$295	4	3
PowerShares Active Low Duration	PLK	$8	0	5
PowerShares 1–30 Laddered Treasury	PLW	$73	1	3
PIMCO Short Term Muni Strategy	SMMU	$13	0	3
PIMCO Intermediate Muni	MUNI	$33	0	3
PIMCO Enhanced Short Maturity	MINT	$179	1	3
PIMCO Broad TIPS	TIPZ	$28	0	3
PIMCO 7–15 Yr Treasury	TENZ	$14	0	3
PIMCO 3–7 Yr Treasury	FIVZ	$50	0	3
PIMCO 25+ Yr Zero Coupon Treasury	ZROZ	$18	0	3
PIMCO 15+ Yr TIPS	LTPZ	$22	0	3
PIMCO 1–5 Yr TIPS	STPZ	$490	2	2
PIMCO 1–3 Yr Treasury	TUZ	$86	0	3
Market Vectors Barclays Pre-Refunded Muni	PRB	$40	0	3

(Continued)

Table A.1 Continued

ETF/ETN Name	Ticker	Net Assets	Share Volume	Ranking
Market Vectors Barclays High Yield Muni	HYD	$159	1	3
Market Vectors Barclays AMT-Free Short Muni	SMB	$89	1	3
Market Vectors Barclays AMT-Free Long Muni	MLN	$34	0	3
Market Vectors Barclays AMT-Free Int Muni	ITM	$159	2	3
iShares S&P/Citi Int'l Treasury	IGOV	$128	0	3
iShares S&P/Citi 1–3 Yr Int'l Treasury	ISHG	$119	0	3
iShares S&P Short Term National Muni	SUB	$352	1	3
iShares S&P National Muni	MUB	$1,833	2	3
iShares S&P California Muni	CMF	$214	0	3
iShares JPM USD Emerging Mkt Bond	EMB	$1,472	4	3
iShares iBoxx Inv Grade Corp Bond	LQD	$12,449	20	3
iShares iBoxx High Yield Corp Bond	HYG	$5,478	19	3
iShares Barclays TIPS	TIP	$20,376	22	2
iShares Barclays Short Treas	SHV	$3,877	12	3
iShares Barclays MBS Bond	MBB	$1,770	2	3
iShares Barclays Intermediate Govt/ Credit	GVI	$458	0	3
iShares Barclays Intermediate Credit	CIU	$2,553	4	3
iShares Barclays Govt/Credit	GBF	$159	0	3
iShares Barclays Credit	CFT	$597	1	3
iShares Barclays Agg	AGG	$11,514	15	3
iShares Barclays Agency	AGZ	$325	0	3
iShares Barclays 7–10 Yr Treas	IEF	$2,711	8	3
iShares Barclays 3–7 Yr Treas	IEI	$941	1	3
iShares Barclays 20+ Yr Treas	TLT	$2,275	104	3
iShares Barclays 1–3 Yr Treas	SHY	$7,823	21	3
iShares Barclays 1–3 Yr Credit	CSJ	$6,253	10	3
iShares Barclays 10–20 Yr Treas	TLH	$263	0	3
iShares 2017 S&P AMT Free Muni	MUAF	$15	0	3
iShares 2016 S&P AMT Free Muni	MUAE	$5	0	5
iShares 2015 S&P AMT Free Muni	MUAD	$15	0	3
iShares 2014 S&P AMT Free Muni	MUAC	$15	0	3
iShares 2013 S&P AMT Free Muni	MUAB	$10	0	5
iShares 2012 S&P AMT Free Muni	MUAA	$10	0	5

Table A.1 Continued

ETF/ETN Name	Ticker	Net Assets	Share Volume	Ranking
iShares 10+ Year Govt/Credit	GLJ	$5	0	5
iShares 10+ Year Credit	CLY	$10	0	5
IndexIQ CPI Inflation	CPI	$14	0	4
Grail McDonnell Intermediate Muni	GMMB	$5	0	5
Grail McDonnell Core Taxable Bond	GMTB	$5	0	5
Direxion Daily 30 Yr Treasury Bull 3×	TMF	$13	1	4
Direxion Daily 2 Yr Treasury Bull 3×	TWOL	$4	0	5
Direxion Daily 10 Yr Treasury Bull 3×	TYD	$7	0	5
Claymore U.S. Capital Markets Bond	UBD	$5	0	5
Claymore U.S. Capital Markets Micro Term Fixed Income	ULQ	$15	0	3
Currency Short				
ProShares UltraShort Yen	YCS	$175	8	4
ProShares UltraShort Euro	EUO	$330	16	4
PowerShares DB US Dollar Index Bearish	UDN	$194	3	3
Market Vectors Double Short Euro ETN	DRR	$58	1	4
Currency Long				
WisdomTree Dreyfus South African Rand	SZR	$11	0	3
WisdomTree Dreyfus New Zealand Dollar	BNZ	$18	0	3
WisdomTree Dreyfus Japanese Yen	JYF	$11	0	3
WisdomTree Dreyfus Indian Rupee	ICN	$32	1	3
WisdomTree Dreyfus Euro	EU	$13	0	3
WisdomTree Dreyfus Emerging Currency	CEW	$435	4	3
WisdomTree Dreyfus Chinese Yuan	CYB	$806	14	3
WisdomTree Dreyfus Brazilian Real	BZF	$159	1	3
Rydex CurrencyShares Swiss Franc Currency	FXF	$304	1	3
Rydex CurrencyShares Swedish Krona Currency	FXS	$34	0	3
Rydex CurrencyShares Russian Ruble Currency	XRU	$7	0	5
Rydex CurrencyShares Pound Sterling Currency	FXB	$130	2	3

(Continued)

Table A.1 Continued

ETF/ETN Name	Ticker	Net Assets	Share Volume	Ranking
Rydex CurrencyShares Mexican Peso Currency	FXM	$45	0	3
Rydex CurrencyShares Japanese Yen Currency	FXY	$211	4	3
Rydex CurrencyShares Euro Currency	FXE	$484	17	3
Rydex CurrencyShares Canadian Dollar Currency	FXC	$599	6	3
Rydex CurrencyShares Australian Dollar Currency	FXA	$726	4	3
ProShares Ultra Yen	YCL	$4	0	5
ProShares Ultra Euro	ULE	$9	0	5
PowerShares DB US Dollar Index Bullish	UUP	$1,400	80	3
PowerShares DB G10 Currency Harvest	DBV	$430	3	5
Market Vectors-Indian Rupee/USD ETN	INR	$7	0	5
Market Vectors-Chinese Renmimbi/ USD ETN	CNY	$39	0	4
Market Vectors Double Long Euro ETN	URR	$4	0	5
iPath Optimized Currency Carry ETN	ICI	$33	0	4
iPath JPY/USD ETN	JYN	$11	0	4
iPath GBP/USD ETN	GBB	$2	0	5
iPath EUR/USD ETN	ERO	$5	0	5
Commodity Short				
U.S. Short Oil	DNO	$20	1	5
ProShares UltraShort Silver	ZSL	$54	17	4
ProShares UltraShort Gold	GLL	$62	6	4
ProShares UltraShort DJ UBS Crude Oil	SCO	$96	58	4
ProShares UltraShort DJ UBS Commodity	CMD	$4	0	5
PowerShares DB Gold Short ETN	DGZ	$22	5	4
PowerShares DB Gold Double Short ETN	DZZ	$67	8	4
PowerShares DB Crude Oil Short ETN	SZO	$9	0	5
PowerShares DB Crude Oil Double Short ETN	DTO	$116	12	4

Table A.1   Continued

ETF/ETN Name	Ticker	Net Assets	Share Volume	Ranking
PowerShares DB Commodity Double Short ETN	DEE	$10	0	5
PowerShares DB Base Metals Short ETN	BOS	$8	0	5
PowerShares DB Base Metals Double Short ETN	BOM	$7	0	5
PowerShares DB Agriculture Short ETN	ADZ	$4	0	5
PowerShares DB Agriculture Double Short ETN	AGA	$9	0	5
E-TRACS UBS Bloomberg CMCI Short Platinum ETN	PTD	$5	0	5
Commodity Long				
U.S. Oil Fund	USO	$1,702	208	5
U.S. Natural Gas	UNG	$2,823	709	5
U.S. Heating Oil	UHN	$15	0	4
U.S. Gasoline	UGA	$98	3	4
U.S. 12 Month Oil	USL	$166	1	4
U.S. 12 Month Natural Gas	UNL	$37	1	4
SPDR Gold	GLD	$43,925	284	2
ProShares Ultra Silver	AGQ	$169	7	4
ProShares Ultra Gold	UGL	$180	4	4
ProShares Ultra DJ UBS Crude Oil	UCO	$172	76	4
ProShares Ultra DJ UBS Commodity	UCD	$13	0	5
PowerShares/DB Agriculture Double Long ETN	DAG	$59	6	4
PowerShares DB Silver	DBS	$66	1	5
PowerShares DB Precious Metals	DBP	$251	4	4
PowerShares DB Oil	DBO	$361	5	4
PowerShares DB Gold Double Long ETN	DGP	$425	21	5
PowerShares DB Gold	DGL	$143	1	4
PowerShares DB Energy	DBE	$344	1	4
PowerShares DB Crude Oil Long ETN	OLO	$16	0	5
PowerShares DB Commodity Short ETN	DDP	$6	0	5
PowerShares DB Commodity Long ETN	DPU	$6	0	5
PowerShares DB Commodity Index	DBC	$4,914	34	4
PowerShares DB Commodity Double Long ETN	DYY	$19	1	5

(Continued)

Table A.1   Continued

ETF/ETN Name	Ticker	Net Assets	Share Volume	Ranking
PowerShares DB Base Metals Long ETN	BDG	$5	0	5
PowerShares DB Base Metals Double Long ETN	BDD	$22	2	4
PowerShares DB Base Metals	DBB	$499	7	5
PowerShares DB Agriculture Long ETN	AGF	$4	0	5
PowerShares DB Agriculture	DBA	$2,328	32	4
Market Vectors Steel	SLX	$417	11	1
iShares Silver Trust	SLV	$5,333	181	2
iShares GSCI Commodity	GSG	$1,790	6	4
iShares COMEX Gold	IAU	$2,982	5	2
iPath S&P GSCI Crude Oil ETN	OIL	$573	13	4
iPath S&P GSCI Commodity ETN	GSP	$101	0	4
iPath DJ AIG Tin ETN	JJT	$3	0	5
iPath DJ AIG Sugar ETN	SGG	$62	2	4
iPath DJ AIG Softs ETN	JJS	$4	0	5
iPath DJ AIG Precious Metals ETN	JJP	$9	0	5
iPath DJ AIG Platinum ETN	PGM	$128	1	4
iPath DJ AIG Nickel ETN	JJN	$31	1	4
iPath DJ AIG Natural Gas ETN	GAZ	$141	5	4
iPath DJ AIG Livestock ETN	COW	$95	1	4
iPath DJ AIG Lead ETN	LD	$5	0	5
iPath DJ AIG Grains ETN	JJG	$109	1	4
iPath DJ AIG Energy ETN	JJE	$25	0	4
iPath DJ AIG Cotton ETN	BAL	$14	0	4
iPath DJ AIG Copper ETN	JJC	$130	2	4
iPath DJ AIG Commodity ETN	DJP	$2,317	7	4
iPath DJ AIG Coffee ETN	JO	$12	0	4
iPath DJ AIG Cocoa ETN	NIB	$12	0	4
iPath DJ AIG Aluminum ETN	JJU	$23	0	4
iPath DJ AIG Agriculture ETN	JJA	$74	0	4
HOLDRs Oil Services	OIH	$2,129	142	1
GS Connect S&P GSCI Enhanced Commodity ETN	GSC	$67	0	4
Greenhaven Continuous Commodity	GCC	$249	1	4
E-TRACS UBS S&P 500 Gold Hedged ETN	SPGH	$12	0	5
E-TRACS UBS DJ-UBS Commodity ETN	DJCI	$14	0	4

Table A.1   Continued

ETF/ETN Name	Ticker	Net Assets	Share Volume	Ranking
E-TRACS UBS Bloomberg CMCI Silver ETN	USV	$4	0	5
E-TRACS UBS Bloomberg CMCI Long Platinum ETN	PTM	$91	1	4
E-TRACS UBS Bloomberg CMCI Livestock ETN	UBC	$9	0	5
E-TRACS UBS Bloomberg CMCI Industrial Metals ETN	UBM	$6	0	5
E-TRACS UBS Bloomberg CMCI Index ETN	UCI	$82	0	4
E-TRACS UBS Bloomberg CMCI Gold ETN	UBG	$5	0	5
E-TRACS UBS Bloomberg CMCI Food ETN	FUD	$6	0	5
E-TRACS UBS Bloomberg CMCI Energy ETN	UBN	$4	0	5
E-TRACS UBS Bloomberg CMCI Agriculture ETN	UAG	$6	0	5
ETFS Silver	SIVR	$137	3	2
ETFS Platinum	PPLT	$607	1	2
ETFS Palladium	PALL	$383	6	2
ETFS Gold	SGOL	$400	1	2
Elements Rogers Int'l Metals ETN	RJZ	$58	1	4
Elements Rogers Int'l Energy ETN	RJN	$53	1	4
Elements Rogers Int'l Commodity Total Return ETN	RJI	$510	8	4
Elements Rogers Int'l Agriculture ETN	RJA	$302	5	4
Elements MLCX Grains ETN	GRU	$16	1	4
Elements MLCX Biofuels ETN	FUE	$2	0	5

SOURCE: National Stock Exchange web site (NSX.com).

Appendix B

Tax Guide for ETF Investors

As the marketing literature from the big fund sponsors constantly reminds us, ETFs are more tax efficient than traditional, actively managed mutual funds. It's true that most of the time, the unique features of ETFs—passive management, stock-like trading on the secondary market, and in-kind redemption of shares by Authorized Participants—give them a tax advantage over mutual funds. However, some ETF investors may be surprised to receive year-end statements from their brokers showing taxable distributions from their exchange-traded funds.

Tax issues for ETFs vary based upon the type of fund and the kind of taxable income it generates. Following is a discussion organized by fund type. This information is not meant to replace advice from financial or tax advisers. Rather, the purpose is to educate investors about tax issues related to certain types of ETFs.

Qualified versus Ordinary Dividends

Many equity-based ETFs pay out dividends to investors. Dividends are popular among investors who are seeking a source of income.

Understanding the tax implications of dividends paid by ETFs, however, can prove challenging.

Under tax relief legislation that is set to expire at the end of 2010, dividends fall into two groups for tax purposes: qualified and ordinary. The tax rate for ordinary dividends is the same as an investor's income tax rate. Qualified dividends for investors in the 25 percent bracket or higher are taxed at 15 percent. Qualified dividends for investors paying an income tax rate of less than 25 percent are taxed at 0 percent.

Certain criteria must be met in order for a dividend to be considered qualified. First, the companies underlying the ETF paying out the income must be American or among a list of qualified foreign companies. Next, the investor must have held the equity for more than 60 days during a 120-day window around the fund's ex-dividend date.

Any dividends that fail to meet these requirements are ordinary dividends. Also considered ordinary dividends are payouts from most real estate investment trusts, or REITs.

Determining how an ETF's distributions are taxed is not always cut-and-dried. As shown in Table B.1, rather than having 100 percent qualified or 100 percent ordinary dividends, in many cases a broad-based index underlying a diversified ETF will include corporations whose dividends are considered qualified and others that are not.

Finally, tax breaks on qualified dividends were initially introduced with the Jobs and Growth Tax Relief Reconciliation Act of 2003 and are set to continue until December 31, 2010. Unless Congress approves

Table B.1 Qualified Dividend Income Percentage

ETF	Qualified Dividend Income % (2009)
iShares S&P 500 Index Fund (IVV)	100%
iShares FTSE NAREIT Residential Plus Capped Index Fund (REZ)	1.27%
iShares Russell 2000 Index Fund (IWM)	64.77%

SOURCE: iShares 2009 Distributions—Year End Tax Supplement Report.

an extension, after this date, all dividends will be taxed as ordinary income.

The best way to determine the qualified/ordinary dividend tax breakdown of your ETF is to visit its respective provider's web site.

Preferred Stock ETFs

Distributions earned from preferred stock ETFs such as iShares S&P U.S. Preferred Stock Index Fund (PFF) are taxed in the same manner as traditional equity-based ETFs, as described above.

Equity Sector Dividends

Another consideration for investors is the particular equity sector they are targeting with ETFs and the dividends that are generated by different types of companies. For example, as Table B.2 shows, sector ETFs that are associated with companies paying dividends—such as

Table B.2 Total Dividend Income (2009) Approx

ETF	Dividend Income per share
iShares Dow Jones U.S. Financial Sector Index Fund (IYF)	$0.88
iShares Dow Jones U.S. Consumer Goods Sector Index Fund (IYK)	$1.34
iShares Dow Jones Transportation Average Index Fund (IYT)	$1.13
iShares Dow Jones U.S. Technology Sector Index Fund (IYW)	$0.26
iShares Dow Jones U.S. Utilities Sector Index Fund (IDU)	$2.78
iShares Dow Jones U.S. Energy Sector Index Fund (IYE)	$0.49
iShares Dow Jones U.S. Real Estate Index Fund (IYR)	$1.93

SOURCE: iShares 2009 Distributions—Year End Tax Supplement Report.

Table B.3   EWZ Distributions

Payable Date	Income	ST Cap Gains	LT Cap Gains
1/6/2010	$0.11	—	—
12/31/2009	$2.19	—	—
6/29/2009	$0.41	—	—
1/5/2009	$0.20	—	—
12/31/2008	$1.32	—	—
6/30/2008	$0.63	—	—
1/4/2008	$0.77	$0.13	$0.30

SOURCE: http://us.ishares.com/product_info/fund/distributions/EWZ.htm.

consumer goods or financial—generate income. Sectors in which companies do not typically make significant payouts, such as technology, have low dividend income. This is yet another consideration for investors as they target investment opportunities in specific sectors.

International

Many international ETFs pay out dividends to investors. However, payouts from international ETFs often vary by amount and frequency. This can make income distribution and tax exposure from these funds unpredictable.

The variation in international ETF payouts is illustrated in Table B.3, which shows distributions from iShares MSCI Brazil Index Fund (EWZ).

The lesson for investors is to be aware of the variation in the size and frequency of the dividends paid by international ETFs, and to plan accordingly with a tax professional.

Exchange-Traded Notes (ETNs)

In the case of equity exchange-traded notes (ETNs)—such as the iPath MSCI India Index ETN (INP)—no dividends are paid to shareholders. With the exception of currency ETNs, these ETNs are considered prepaid contracts. Therefore, investors record a gain or loss when they sell the fund. This amount is then taxed as capital gains based on how long the investor held the security.

A unique ETN example is the J.P. Morgan Alerian MLP Index ETN (AMJ). This ETN tracks an index of master limited partnerships (MLPs). Gains and losses from partnerships are taxed at the individual level, so they pass through to the investor. An investor who owns individual MLPs will generally receive a K-1 form, instead of a 1099, for reporting losses and gains from a partnership. AMJ pays out quarterly distributions, although it reports using a 1099 form.

MLPs are popular with income investors due to their high yield. However, investors may not like having to deal with the greater complexity of a K-1 if they do their own taxes. In some cases, individuals may find their taxes are lower if they own the MLPs individually. As with other areas of complexity, it makes sense to consult a tax professional to determine which approach is most suitable for you.

Fixed Income ETFs

Investors can use ETFs to gain exposure to Treasuries, corporate bonds, municipal bonds, international bonds, and even Build America Bonds. Because these products expose investors to different types of debt securities, there are a few noticeable differences in the ways they are taxed.

As with equity-based funds, bond ETFs are designed in a manner that typically exempts shareholders from paying capital gains taxes until the shares are sold. However, as illustrated by Table B.4, there are events that trigger capital gains on bond ETFs.

Table B.4   2009 Year-End Capital Gains Distributions

ETF	Approx % of NAV
iShares 1–3 Year Treasury Bond Fund (SHY)	0.59%
iShares 3–7 Year Treasury Bond Fund (IEI)	0.27%
iShares 1–3 Year Credit Bond Fund (CSJ)	0.00%

Source: http://us.ishares.com/topics/2009_capital_gains.htm.

Income collected from U.S. Treasury-linked ETFs, such as the iShares 1–3 Year Treasury Bond Fund (SHY), are generally exempt from state and local taxes. However, federal taxes still apply.

Payouts from municipal bond-backed ETFs, such as the iShares S&P National Municipal Bond Fund (MUB), are typically exempt from federal taxes. Additionally, there are a handful of single-state-focused municipal bond funds such as the iShares S&P California AMT-Free Municipal Bond Fund (CMF), which pay out income that is exempt from California income tax. CMF and many other municipal bond funds are also designed to hold bonds that are exempt from the federal alternative minimum tax.

The PowerShares Build America Bond Portfolio (BAB), as the name implies, provides investors with exposure to Build America Bonds. These debt securities are taxable municipal bonds issued by state and local governments that have their interest subsidized by the U.S. Treasury. Like other muni bond ETFs, the income earned from BAB is exempt from federal income taxes.

By contrast, distributions from corporate bond ETFs, such as the iShares iBoxx $ Investment Grade Corporate Bond Fund (LQD), are taxed as ordinary income.

Investors holding international bond ETFs may be subject to foreign income taxes. Determining what those taxes may be, however, is difficult. The taxes would be withheld from investors, who may then be eligible for a foreign tax credit. For instance, SPDR Barclays Capital International Treasury Bond ETF (BWX) offers a breakdown of the foreign sources of income and foreign tax credit eligibility. In 2009, 100 percent of the income was eligible. Not all investors may be eligible for the credit, however. Therefore, it's advisable to check with a tax professional.

Capital Gains

ETFs are generally able to do a better job of deferring capital gains taxes until the sale of the fund. Nonetheless, investors will be responsible for capital gains based on how long they held the ETF, the same as they would with an individual stock.

While investors holding a passively managed ETF can usually avoid paying capital gains tax before they sell, as the industry evolves a greater number of actively managed ETFs are being launched. In addition, some unique strategies being deployed by new types of funds may be more likely to result in capital gains distributions.

For instance, in 2009 one of PowerShares' unique instruments, the PowerShares NASDAQ-100 BuyWrite Portfolio (PQBW), which writes covered calls on the NASDAQ 100 index, realized a 15 percent capital gains distribution. Further, it is likely that a fund such as the IndexIQ ARB Merger Arbitrage ETF (MNA) could see capital gains distributions in the future. According to IndexIQ's web site, MNA is designed to track companies around the globe that have been announced as takeover targets. Given this focus, there could be a large amount of index turnover, which, in turn, could lead to capital gains.

Keep in mind that although actively managed ETFs are more likely to have capital gains distributions in the future, they still carry tax advantages compared to mutual funds.

While ETF providers work hard to reduce capital gains, distributions still occur at times. At the end of 2009, two Van Eck international products, Market Vectors Brazil Small Cap ETF (BRF) and Market Vectors Vietnam ETF (VNM), generated short-term capital gains. Additionally, in May 2010, five of Van Eck's municipal bond–focused funds also generated distributions.

Currency ETFs

Investors can gain exposure to international currencies using a wide variety of exchange-traded products. While every currency product attempts to achieve a similar objective, their tax implications are not uniform. In addition, there is a key difference in the treatment of currency ETNs and other types of ETNs, as previously described.

An example of a popular currency ETF is Rydex's CurrencyShares Euro Trust ETF (FXE), which tracks the performance of a physical basket of euros. These products make monthly income distributions that are subject to ordinary income tax. What may come as a surprise to investors, however, is that an instrument like FXE is not subject to long- or short-term capital gains tax because the IRS considers all currency gains as ordinary income, rather than capital gains.

Unlike other ETNs, currency ETNs are subject to the same tax treatment as currency ETFs. One key difference with an ETN, such as iPath EUR/USD Exchange Rate ETN (ERO), however, is that the fund does not pay out income distributions. Rather, income earned from the holdings underlying ERO will be reinvested in the fund. Although the income is not paid to the holder, the holder is still required to pay income tax on income earned by the fund during the year. This could catch some investors off-guard. Furthermore, given that the ETN structure comes with credit risk, it may make more sense for investors to stick with ETFs to gain currency exposure.

In addition, a group of ETNs use a strategy known as the carry trade. These funds short the currencies that have the lowest interest rates and buy the currencies with the highest interest rates. This does have some tax implications. According to Barclays, holders of its iPath Optimized Currency Carry ETN (ICI) do not have to recognize current income as they do with ERO and other currency ETNs; however, when they sell, their gains are taxed as ordinary income, the same as the other currency ETNs.

Other examples of currency ETFs include WisdomTree's offerings. Its Japanese yen and euro ETFs track debt securities denominated in the respective foreign currency. Emerging market products, such as the WisdomTree Chinese Yuan Fund (CYB), track U.S. money market securities as well as swaps and forward currency contracts. As with CurrencyShares' and iPath's products, any income generated from these products will be taxed as ordinary income. As stated on the WisdomTree web site, gains in the fund will be taxed as ordinary income, but if eligible for mark-to-market treatment, taxation is based on 60 percent long-term capital gain and 40 percent short-term capital gain. Investors would need to consult a tax professional to determine whether or not that eligibility applies.

A final group of currency ETFs is a futures-based product. The popular PowerShares DB U.S. Dollar Bullish Fund (UUP) and its inverse, the Bearish Fund (UDN), track U.S. Dollar Index futures. Capital gains are taxed as 60 percent long-term gains and 40 percent short-term, regardless of how long the investor holds the fund. This type of ETF is structured as a partnership and investors will receive a K-1 form at tax time. (For more information, see the discussion of futures-backed ETFs under the commodities section.)

Commodity ETFs

Over the past several years, a host of new ETFs from State Street, Barclays, PowerShares, Rydex, WisdomTree, and other fund sponsors have opened up markets that previously were difficult for individual investors to access. Asset classes such as commodities, foreign real estate, and currencies that used to be open primarily to institutional or high-net-worth investors have become accessible to nearly everyone with a brokerage account. While these new ETFs have provided investors with myriad opportunities to diversify their portfolios, they have also brought some surprising—and not altogether welcome—tax consequences.

Unlike ETFs built on traditional equity or bond indexes, funds that hold currencies, futures contracts, or hard assets such as precious metals receive different treatment under the U.S. tax code. Individuals looking to diversify into these areas need to know the sometimes arcane tax rules that govern these asset classes before they decide to commit their investment dollars.

Precious Metals

For investors seeking exposure to the precious metals markets, exchange-traded funds offer several ways to go. The most direct exposure can be found in funds that hold physical gold and silver bullion, such as SPDR Gold Shares (GLD). Others, such as the PowerShares DB Silver Fund (DBS), use futures contracts to gain precious metals exposure and are taxed the same as futures contracts. There are also precious metals ETNs that face yet another tax implication.

When it comes to physical gold and silver, the IRS takes a unique taxation approach. The tax code classifies metals—whether in the form of ingots, jewelry, or coins—as "collectibles" and applies a specific set of rules. Under the tax code as it currently stands, gains recognized from the sale of collectibles, including gold and silver (the rules also apply to art, antiques, and other items) held for more than one year are taxed at a maximum rate of 28 percent. The maximum rate on short-term gains—that is, capital gains recognized upon the sale of assets held for one year or less—is generally the same as the shareholder's income tax rate.

Investors who purchase ETFs that directly own precious metals should factor this into their overall investment strategy. One way to defer this tax bite is to hold precious metals ETFs in a tax-deductible IRA or a Roth IRA.

Futures

Another way to gain exposure to precious metals is with funds that use gold or silver futures contracts. Examples of this strategy are PowerShares DB Gold Fund (DGL) and PowerShares DB Silver Fund (DBS). Keep in mind, though, ETFs that use futures contracts to achieve their results, whether they track gold, silver, corn, copper, or currencies, come with their own tax twist.

Futures contracts are taxed under a mark-to-market system. This is where things can get a little tricky, and where investors who hold futures-linked ETFs need to be careful. Under the terms of the tax code, futures contracts held at the end of the taxable year will be treated for federal income tax purposes as if they were sold at their fair market value. The net gains or losses resulting from these so-called deemed sales, along with the net gain or loss from any actual sales, must be taken into account by the ETF when it determines its taxable income for the year. ETF shareholders are on the hook for their pro rata share of the taxes on this income.

Many commodity ETF investors are no doubt shocked when they receive a K-1 tax form in the mail. Most futures-based funds are set up as partnerships, and investors are taxed on gains and losses in the proportion of 60 percent long-term capital gains and 40 percent short-term capital gains, whether they sold the fund or not. These forms can be a headache for individuals doing their own taxes, and many investors may not like having a tax liability on a fund they have yet to sell.

As always, one way investors can mitigate adverse tax consequences is by holding futures-based ETFs in tax-deferred accounts.
Investors who purchase futures-backed ETFs in an IRA, for instance,
can avoid the associated tax liability. The investor will still be issued
a K-1 form, though, and should save it for record keeping.

Another way around the different taxation for futures-backed
commodity ETFs is to use ETNs. While ETNs carry credit risk, they
also offer a third option for investors concerned about tax liability
because their capital gains are taxed like equity ETFs, at a rate based
on how long the individual has held the fund. In some cases there
are one-to-one index substitutes for a fund, such as PowerShares DB
Commodity (DBC) and PowerShares DB Commodity ETN (DPU),
but they may have very different liquidity. For example, DPU recently
traded only 5,000 shares per day, while DBC traded 1.8 million. In
other cases, there may not be a one-to-one substitute. As with any
investment decision, remember that the suitability of the investment
is primary and tax implications are secondary.

Leveraged ETFs

ETFs designed to provide investors with magnified or inverse exposure to a specific index are typically considered less tax efficient than
traditional ETFs. Rather than tracking a basket of exchange-traded
securities, products such as the Direxion Daily Financial Bull 3X (FAS)
and the Short QQQ ProShares (PSQ) invest in derivative instruments
including futures, swaps, and forwards in an effort to achieve their
specific goals.

Since the vast majority of holders of these funds are traders, they
tend to move in and out of the products quickly. If more investors
are leaving the fund than are coming in, the fund's assets will dip,
requiring the provider to sell some of the derivative products underlying the fund.

As illustrated in Table B.5, when the markets were wildly volatile
at the end of 2008, large short-term capital gains were generated for
a number of ProShares' Short and UltraShort ETF products.

These funds are able to achieve their objective with a small amount
of capital. The rest of the fund's assets are invested in interest-bearing

Table B.5   ProShares Capital Gains (Q4 2008)

ETF	4th Quarter 2008 Dividend (approx.)	4th Quarter 2008 ST Cap Gains (approx.)	4th Quarter 2008 LT Cap Gains (approx.)
ProShares UltraShort Russell MidCap Value (SJL)	—	$50.35	—
ProShares UltraShort Industrials (SIJ)	$0.05	$47.84	—
ProShares UltraShort Semiconductors (SSG)	$0.04	$42.34	—
ProShares UltraShort Financials (SKF)	—	—	—
ProShares Short S&P 500 (SH)	—	$11.94	$0.04
ProShares Short Dow 30 (DOG)	$0.03	$8.44	$0.27
ProShares UltraShort Oil & Gas (DUG)	$0.02	$6.06	—

SOURCE: http://www.proshares.com/funds/#sort=Name&tab=distributions.

securities. Any income that may be earned from leveraged equity ETFs are taxed as ordinary income.

Income generated from a leveraged bond ETF such as ProShares Short 20+ Year Treasury Bond Fund (TBT) is subject to federal income tax.

Come tax time, leveraged currency and commodity ETFs from ProShares are treated in the same fashion as unleveraged commodities ETFs. Because they are treated as a partnership, investors holding ProShares Ultra Gold (UGL) receive the K-1 tax form. Gains and losses from UGL's underlying holdings will face the same capital gains ratios of 60 percent long term and 40 percent short term.

As stated previously in the book, leveraged ETFs typically reset daily and should only be held for short periods of time. Furthermore, these funds are best suited for professional traders and highly experienced traders.

APPENDIX C

Growth of the ETF Industry from 2000 to 2009

S ince first making their appearance, the popularity of exchange traded funds has taken off. With nearly 2,000 products trading on exchanges across the globe and more than $1 trillion in assets under management, it is clear that ETFs are becoming more commonplace among average retail investors. As the industry continues to expand and provide access to new, previously unattainable areas of the global economy, this trend of growth is only expected to continue.

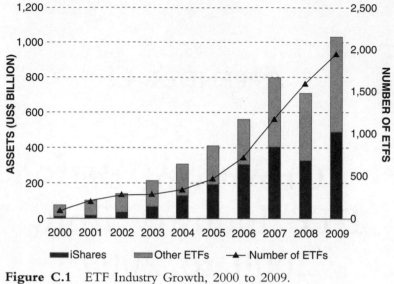

Figure C.1   ETF Industry Growth, 2000 to 2009.
Source: http://au.ishares.com/publish/content/images/get_started/aum_growth.gif.

APPENDIX D

Sample Model Portfolios

This appendix presents a sample portfolio for each of the trader/investor profiles introduced in Chapter 4:

- The Super Hands-On Active Trader
- The High-Touch Satellite Investor
- The Portfolio Builder
- The Core Holder
- The Armchair Investor
- The Autopilot Investor

The Super Hands-On Active Trader

The Super Hands-On Active Trader is a professional who uses ETFs to hedge a position or to gain exposure intraday. The key phrase here is *intraday*. The Super Hands-On Active Trader is moving into and out of funds within a single trading day and may use leveraged funds that seek to deliver double or triple the performance of a particular index.

ETF	Symbol	% Weighting
Direxion Financial Bull 3X	FAS	25
ProShares Ultra QQQ	QLD	25
Direxion Daily Emerging Markets 3X	EDC	25
Direxion Daily Small Cap Bull 3X	TNA	25

The High-Touch Satellite Investor

The next type of investor definitely takes an active approach, seeking exposure to particular sectors—such as software, e-commerce, consumer goods, and so on. These types of ETFs are appealing for their ease of entry, relatively low fees, and liquidity. This investor will favor funds that have low fees and high liquidity.

ETF	Symbol	% Weighting
iShares Dow Consumer Goods	IYK	10
iShares Software	IGV	10
iShares DJ US Basic Materials	IYM	10
First Trust DJ Internet Index	FDN	10
SPDR Gold Shares	GLD	10
iShares Morningstar Large Core	JKD	10
iShares DJ US Financial Sector	RFG	10
iShares DJ Select Dividend	DVY	10
Vanguard Emerging Markets	EEM	10
iShares DJ Medical Devices	IHI	10

The Portfolio Builder

This next type of investor seeks to build a complete portfolio using ETFs. It may be that this investor has a nest egg to invest or has a portfolio to rebuild after being all or mostly in cash during a market downturn, such as we experienced during the 2007–2008 financial crisis. As we will discuss, the Portfolio Builder includes three subcategories of investors who use ETFs to construct their portfolio, but with an increasingly hands-off approach. They are the Core Holder, the Armchair Investor, and the Autopilot Investor.

ETF	Symbol	% Weighting
SPDR S&P 500	SPY	15
PowerShares QQQ Trust	QQQQ	10
iShares S&P 500 Value Index	IVE	10
Vanguard Mid-Cap Growth	VOT	10
iShares Russell 2000	IWM	5
Dow Diamonds Trust	DIA	10
Vanguard Total World	VT	10
SPDR Gold Trust	GLD	5
iShares Silver Trust	SLV	5
Vanguard Total Bond Market	BND	5
iShares Barclays TIPS Bond	TIP	5
iShares iBoxx Investment Grade	LQD	10

The Core Holder

This is the first subcategory of Portfolio Builder that we will discuss. The Core Holder typically owns 12 to 16 ETFs, with broad-based funds such as the SPY, DIA, or the QQQQ as core holdings. Although this investor is hands-off—trading very infrequently—he or she needs to understand what these core holdings represent; for example, that the DIA will track the Dow components and the QQQQ is very heavily weighted toward technology.

ETF	Symbol	% Weighting
SPDR S&P 500	SPY	10
PowerShares QQQ Trust	QQQQ	10
Dow Diamonds Trust	DIA	10
SPDR Health Care Sector	IXV	5
iShares Russell 2000	IWM	10
Vanguard REIT	RMZ	5
Vanguard Emerging Market	VWO	10
Market Vectors Agribusiness	MOO	5
SPDR Financial Sector	IXM	5
SPDR Industrial Sector	IXI	5
Vanguard Short-Term Bond	SHM	10
iShares BC 1–3 Year Treasury	SHY	15

The Armchair Investor

A second subcategory within Portfolio Builder is the Armchair Investor. Like the Core Holder, the Armchair Investor holds broad-based ETFs to gain exposure to the major indexes. However, the Armchair Investor is less involved on a regular basis than the Core Holder.

ETF	Symbol	% Weighting
SPDR S&P 500	SPY	15
PowerShares QQQ Trust	QQQQ	10
Dow Diamonds Trust	DIA	10
Vanguard Mid-Cap Growth	VOT	10
Vanguard Total World	VT	15
iShares Russell 3000	IWV	10
Vanguard Short-Term Bond	SHM	10
Vanguard Total Bond Market	BND	15
iShares BC 1–3 Year Treasury	SHY	15

The Autopilot Investor

This last type of Portfolio Builder investor is the least active in his or her own portfolio management. Autopilot Investors use ETFs but are most likely to do so as part of a buy-and-hold approach. They typically use funds that track the broad-based indexes as well as those that have a particular investment style such as large-cap growth or international.

ETF	Symbol	% Weighting
First Trust Large Cap Core AlphaDEX	FEX	15
PowerShares Dyn Market	PWC	25
Rydex S&P 500 Pure Value Growth	RPG	25
PowerShares Dyn Mid Cap Growth	PWJ	15
PowerShares Dyn Developed Int	PFA	10
PowerShares DWA Em Mkts Tech	PIE	10

About the Authors

Don Dion is president and founder of Dion Money Management, a fee-based investment advisory firm to affluent individuals, families, and nonprofit organizations, where he is responsible for setting investment policy, creating custom portfolios, and overseeing the performance of client accounts. Founded in 1996 and based in Williamstown, Massachusetts, Dion Money Management manages assets for clients in 49 states and 11 countries. He is a licensed attorney in Massachusetts and Maine and has more than 25 years' experience working in the financial markets, having founded and run two publicly traded companies before establishing Dion Money Management.

Dion also is publisher of the Fidelity Independent Adviser family of newsletters, which provides to a broad range of investors his commentary on the financial markets, with a specific emphasis on mutual funds and exchange-traded funds. With more than 100,000 subscribers in the United States and 29 other countries, Fidelity Independent Adviser publishes six monthly newsletters and three weekly newsletters. Its flagship publication, *Fidelity Independent Adviser*, has been published monthly for 11 years and reaches 40,000 subscribers.

Carolyn Dion is an analyst and associate editor for the Fidelity
Independent Adviser family of newsletters, Dion Money Management's
affiliate newsletter company. A former ETF specialist and NYSE Arca
lead market maker, she provides analysis on the exchange-traded
product industry.

In addition to her role as analyst and editor, Carolyn is vice president
of Dion Money Management, a fee-based investment advisory
firm, where she assists in the development of ETF strategies. Founded
in 1996 and based in Williamstown, Massachusetts, Dion Money
Management manages more than $530 million in assets for clients in
49 states and 11 countries.

Before joining Dion Money Management, Carolyn worked as an
ETF market maker for Kellogg Specialist Group on the New York
Stock Exchange and American Stock Exchange. She received a bachelor's
degree from Bowdoin College in Brunswick, Maine.

Index